TRAVELS T⊤ ⌐A
W⌐

ROGER D. TAYLOR

TRAVELS THROUGH A WINDOW

To Nigel & Teresa.

A little memento of Ardamerton ...

with best wishes.

31st October 2023

THE FITZROY PRESS

Cover illustration: Roger D Taylor
Published by The FitzRoy Press 2023.

$\mathcal{F}$
The FitzRoy Press
9 Regent Gate
Waltham Cross
Herts EN8 7AF

ISBN 978 1739214 203

A catalogue record for this book is available from the British Library

Publishing management by Troubador Publishing Ltd, Leicestershire, UK
Printed and bound in the UK by TJ Books Limited, Padstow, Cornwall

For Zephy, Carnaby and Quinna

Mise mar riut 's mi 'nam ònar
ag amharc fuachd na linne còmnhaird,
a'cluintinn onfhaidh air faolinn
bristeadh air leacan loma 'n t-saoghail.

Somhairle MacGill-Eain, *A' Chorra- Ghridheach*

I am with you, alone,
gazing at the coldness of the level kyle,
listening to the surge on a stony shore
breaking on the bare flagstones of the world.

Sorley Maclean, *The Heron*

1

My window is five feet eight inches wide and four feet ten inches high. Beneath the window on the inside wall there is a radiator, and hard against that is my writing table. With both its leaves open the table is almost as wide as the window. In the middle is my laptop computer, on which I am writing. The table has a single folding wooden chair.

On the table, as well as the computer, and working roughly from left to right are:

A yacht's anchor light.

A stone marmalade jar, James Keiller & Sons, Dundee, Grand Medal of Merit Vienna 1873, and Only Prize Medal for Marmalade, London 1862, containing a yellow HB pencil and a Pentel Fine Point pen.

A copy of *A Field Guide to the Birds of Britain and Europe*, by Peterson, Mountfort and Hollom, 3rd Revised Edition 1958.

A copy of *Letters from a Stoic, Epistulae Morales ad Lucilium*, by Seneca, Penguin Classics 2004.

A Blue Domino fruit bowl in which is one apple, a red delicious.

A copy of *Meditations*, by Marcus Aurelius.

The ship's log for my most recent voyage, open at Day 44, Saturday 16th August 2014.

The informal notebook for the same voyage.

Three assorted candlesticks, two with candles in them.

A woven rush place mat.

Admiralty Chart 5616-18, in a clear plastic sleeve, showing Kyle Akin, Loch Alsh and Upper Loch Carron.

A computer mouse.

A pair of Opticron DBA 10 x 42 binoculars.

A French enamelled coffee percolator, also in Blue Domino. Near the bottom of the percolator is a rust patch with a hole in it.

An Ordnance Survey map: 428 Kyle of Lochalsh, Plockton & Applecross.

A late spring snowstorm passes through, frosting the slopes and pine forests of Meall Ailein, just across the loch. Further back, the peak of Beinn Conchra, faintly visible in the crook of two opposing ridges, has turned almost pure white.

*

A mistle thrush is feeding on the grass that sweeps down sixty yards or so to the loch edge. Its breast and underparts are heavily blotched. It hops three or four times and cocks its head, listening for worms.

The wind is now in the south-west, fresh and cold. I start to form a phrase that might capture the texture and movement of the water, but it is lost as I reach for the binoculars. It is a male merganser, heading seawards. Its mate follows. I have just put down the binoculars when I need them again. A party of eider ducks lands to the east of the Strome Islands. From my window the islands look like a single outcrop, but at high water it divides into three. The long streak of rock, covered at its highest point by vegetation and a few stunted trees, lies about a third of the way across the loch, to my right.

The surface of the loch is roughing up. I can hear the wind buffeting the house. A flock of meadow pipits sweeps across, driven on by the squall. I can see rain now, or possibly sleet, scudding through the valley behind Creag an Duilisg. It draws across like a final curtain, hiding the more distant hills. Within a few seconds it is gone as if it were never there. The loch sparkles.

Now I can see the full height of the clouds. They are fulsome thunderheads, moving quickly. Higher up a layer of wispy cirrus restrains the blue of the clear patch.

The clouds keep coming, on and on.

*

My hands are cold. I could lean over and switch on the oil heater, but I prefer things as they are. On the edge of discomfort I feel alive. My cold hands match the hard chair on which I am sitting.

I stare through the window. It is half tide. Rocks and patches of seaweed lie above the water's edge. I am not immediately sure whether it is the flood or the ebb, although I am a sailor and I ought to know.

I stare a while longer, waiting for words that refuse to come. For a second or two I feel the peace of a head empty of language.

The silence is almost perfect. It is marred only by a slight ringing in my left ear and the whirr of the computer. Perhaps

I should write by hand. Or perhaps not write at all. I wonder about endless choices which are not really choices.

The Plockton train passes: two carriages from Inverness. It rolls along the other side of the loch from left to right, over the Fernaig railway bridge, and out of sight. I can still hear it: *clunkity-dunk, clunkity-dunk, clunkity-dunk.*

The breeze this morning is light and from the east and barely troubles the surface of the loch. Had I a little sailing boat I could cross to the other side and look back at my window. Perhaps I could wave to myself.

A jet engine, somewhere aloft, cuts across the purr of my computer. I look up and see that the clouds are coming from the south-west. The east wind on the loch is fading. The water is dotted with calm patches. Had I sailed across the loch I may have had to row back.

*

The morning sun has climbed into the top left-hand corner of my window. I shield my face with my left hand and continue typing with one finger. If I sit right back in my chair the horizontal wooden glazing bar hides the sun from my eyes and I can type with both hands, arms outstretched. A cloud from the east resolves the problem.

I re-phrase the first sentence. It really should be: *the top left-hand corner of my window has rotated into alignment with the sun.*

I am not sitting here tapping at a keyboard. I am travelling. I too have rotated into alignment with the sun. I will continue rotating all day, at great speed.

I try some mathematics. Using the Admiralty Chart by my right elbow I check the latitude of my window. It is 57° 21' 30" North. I calculate that the length of this line of latitude is about 7,600 miles. That is the distance that I and my window rotate every day. Had I lived my whole life at this window I would by now have travelled 70 x 365 x 7,600 miles: almost 195 million. This does not take account of the forward motion of the planet, or leap years, or the fact that I have not quite arrived at my birth date.

I resolve never again to submit to the illusion that the sun orbits the earth. I inhabit a spinning sphere. I have travelled more than three hundred miles since finishing my bowl of porridge.

I sit at my window, attentive to the journey.

*

The wind is from the east.

Across the loch are two waterside houses, about two or three hundred yards apart. One is slightly to the right of the midline of my window, towards the Fernaig railway bridge, the other slightly to the left. A red car leaves the driveway of the right hand house and drives slowly along the track to the left hand house. I follow it with my binoculars. The driver gets out and opens the double gates of the left hand house's driveway. The driver's manner suggests it is a woman. She parks the car inside the gates and carries two large bags into the house. The whole sequence takes two and a half minutes.

*

Behind the two houses, on the far side of the railway line, is a steep slope, about sixty feet high. It is covered in birch trees not yet in leaf. A firebreak runs up the slope just to the right of the left hand house. The firebreak is bare, but the ridge above it is thick with yellow gorse. I realise that I have never noticed the firebreak or the gorse. Now that I know they are there I can look at nothing else. The red car is parked directly below the firebreak, beside the left hand house, but for the moment it holds no interest. I would like to walk up the firebreak, to examine its gradient and its vegetation. I wonder whether the gorse is confined to the ridge, or whether it extends down the other side. I am unlikely ever to walk up the firebreak, and so I can choose whichever option I prefer without fear of error.

*

The waves on the loch are pulsing obliquely into the shoreline below my window. It is just after high tide and so I cannot see them breaking on the pebbles; the edge of the water is hidden by the grassy bank at the bottom of the croft.

I examine the waves. They are not unlike pelagic waves. Their shape and texture are as they should be. Some tumble forward in a convincing manner, but the timing is wrong: the crests pass every second or so. This is a function of their scale and means that however much I stare at them they will never transport me back to the open sea.

*

An orange mass, partly hidden by fence posts and bare shrubs, moves into the lower right segment of my window. It is a sit-on mower driven by my neighbour. It bumps along the grassy track above the shoreline and turns into the ungated entrance at the bottom of the croft. It stops and reverses out with opposite lock to face the other way along the track. My neighbour is wearing a Norfolk jacket, goggles, corduroy trousers and green Wellington boots. He engages forward gear and the mower sets off back along the track. Within four seconds it is out of sight.

*

Rain blurs the window, distorting everything. The drops do not run down vertically, but at a slight angle, pushed by the wind. By lining up a rivulet I can make the right hand house across the loch lose its front door. I can do the same with the left hand house but that is less amusing. The left hand house is bigger and still has a red car parked beside it, in line with the firebreak and the gorse.

Despite the low cloud, Beinn Conchra pushes up above the most distant ridge. As well as being the furthest visible peak, it is exactly in the middle of my window, on the horizontal plane. On my window ledge is a four point stag's antler which I found on the upper croft. Beinn Conchra is directly above the antler's second point, which is thirty-four inches from each side of the window.

On the window ledge, from left to right, are:

A candlestick with a candle in it.
A yacht's steaming light.
An antique Parisian candle holder cum cigar lighter.
A four point stag's antler.
A small brass oil lamp.
An antique cigarette lighter.
A shoehorn fashioned from a bull's horn.

I wait for the rain to come on more strongly. I would like to track the degrees of distortion the rain could cause.

At the edge of the loch a herring gull tugs at seaweed.

The rain eases and I decide that I would prefer Beinn Conchra not to be centred so precisely. It is a little too neat.

The window is now clear except for the occasional drop. Beinn Conchra has disappeared into the cloud.

*

I have not opened the right hand curtain far enough. It is olive green with a gold tinge and patterned with striped vertical spirals and dots. The curtain is obscuring part of my view, hiding the western end of the Strome Islands and the highest point of Creag an Duilisg. I cannot decide whether to get up to correct the imbalance, or whether to live with it as an experiment.

My thinking is interrupted by a blue workboat, the *Toohey II*, which powers its way seaward against wind and tide, crossing my line of sight from left to right. On its deck is a wooden garden bench.

Two goldfinches perch briefly on the low shrub just in front of my window.

I make a decision. I will get up and open the curtain fully. The more I think about the curtain hiding a segment of my field of view, the more intolerable it becomes.

2

It is nearly three weeks: motorways, cities, aeroplanes, people; motion going nowhere. I slough off the noise and dirt and move back towards equilibrium. A wheatear flicks his white rump along the bottom fence. I sit perfectly still, eyes centred on Beinn Conchra. It is calming, to spin in phase with a mountain peak, its solidity as illusory as mine.

Momentary sunshine lights up the grass of the meadow still wringing from this morning's shower. Our angle of travel has changed, pushing the sun above the window lintel. The sunlight no longer troubles my eyes but falls warmly on the back of my hands.

I am still unsettled. It will take another day or two to re-establish the rhythm of the road.

*

A chance opposition of the flood tide against a faint breeze from the east makes the waves dance just a few yards off the water's edge. The shimmering movement is impossible to follow: every second a thousand wavelets push up and subside. The air is heavy with low cloud, so there is no sparkle; the play of the water is defined by nothing more than weak shadow.

A catalogue of memories forms unbidden in my mind, images of similar dancing waves in distant seas. I suppress past life. It is gone, if it were ever there. I suspect it may be a canker, gnawing away at the purity of the present. Perhaps it was all a false journey, the wrong route to the wrong destination.

I make another resolution: to strip away all I have seen and learned. I do not know whether this is possible; whether an aging man can rediscover innocence.

*

A fledgling pied wagtail is standing in the lee of a low clump of privet, twenty feet in front of my window, waiting to be fed. It looks around, anxiously. I wonder how it interprets what it sees. It will never learn to name things: Cat, Dog, Mummy, Moo-cow, Mountain, Water, House, Window. It takes off and flies straight towards me. For a moment I think that it is going to hit the glass that separates us. It veers upwards out of sight, fluttering, by the looks of it, onto the guttering.

*

My right shoulder is aching, drawing my concentration away from the view. It is only my body, a tiresome counterpart, but the pain is insistent. I speculate as to what mental diversion it would take to over-ride it: a sea eagle landing on the bottom fencepost; a red car exploding across the loch; a procession of wimpled nuns along the shoreline. In the hierarchy of pleasure and pain, anything can be trumped.

Another book has appeared on my table: *Meditations on First Philosophy, with Selections from the Objections and Replies*, by René Descartes, translated by John Cottingham, with an introduction by Bernard Williams, Cambridge University Press 1986.

I examine the terraced profile of Creag Mhaol, the buttress of tortured rock, tree-clad in parts, which dominates the left middle ground of my view. Its mass steadies my mind, allowing me to search within myself for Descartes' *a priori* idea of God. I find no hint; nothing. I have to admit the possibility that this is down to a defect in myself. Perhaps my prejudice is too strong, or my imagination too stunted.

A siskin flicks across the window, a ball of green and yellow, whisked on by the wind.

I formulate a question: *if my mind cannot grasp the idea of God, and if God is my creator, how can I be at fault?*

The tide is falling away, leaving shallow water almost to the Strome Islands. The seabed of hard sand patched with rock and seaweed is tinged lime green in the early afternoon sun. A small seal splashes its way seawards.

*

I feel tired; weary to the marrow. A red-throated diver flies high across the loch, silhouetted against unmoving grey cloud, but it does not stir me. I realise that to sit so still, day after day, trying to draw the essence out of water, rock, tree, grass, sky, bird, white house, red car, spinning planet and so on and so forth *ad infinitum*, is a hard lot. It may kill me. There is nothing else to be done.

*

Two greylag geese are feeding on the grass at the bottom of the croft, in the open gateway. They wander out towards the shore, working their way to my right.

There is no wind, and for once I can see the movement of the water as the tide ebbs. The whole loch is a broad stream, flowing westwards. I think of the full moon glimpsed the previous night but immediately suppress the image; I may only have dreamed it. I concentrate instead on the mechanics of the present moment: the water and I spinning *en masse* towards the east, but the water also falling towards the west, at a much slower speed. It would be amusing to be out on the loch right now, drifting with the tide, knowing that my rate of spin is reduced by the pull of a hidden moon.

Three more geese fly in from the loch and land at the bottom of the croft, the white of their tail feathers freshly starched and luminous.

＊

Something is not quite right about the view; somewhere a detail is lacking. It gnaws away at me, a lost word on the tip of my tongue. My eye ranges around but finds nothing. I decide to be systematic, working from large to small. The mountains are all present and correct: Creag Mhaol to my left, Creag an Duilisg to my right, between them Meall Ailein stretching away to Beinn Conchra. The loch has not drained away. I count the houses across the loch: one, two, three, four, five, six: no overnight demolitions. The Fernaig railway bridge is still standing. I can see no sign of sudden forest clearances. I sense that the difference is somewhere in my direct line of sight. I study the house across the loch, slightly to left of centre. Behind it is the firebreak topped by gorse. I follow the firebreak down to the right of the house. I see now that the red car has gone.

*

The hills across the loch are misted by the rain driving in from the south-west. Waves break against the seaward end of the Strome Islands, sending momentary plumes of white spray skywards.

I watch two greylag geese fly from this side of the loch to the other. It takes them only forty seconds to reach the far shore. For a moment I envy them their speed and ease of movement.

*

The red car is back. I analyse the colours presently in view: various greens, a pewter-blue loch, violet-grey clouds, a few patches of yellow gorse. Only the red car, parked where it should be, and a small patch of purple rhododendron on the Strome Islands, introduce two bolder smears to the scene. In the fading light they too lose their distinctness.

I sit and watch our journey into the night as we spin away from the sun.

The greens grow more sombre. Even the grass in front of my window has lost its freshness. The pine plantations on Meall Ailein are almost black. The pines bristle along the topmost ridge

The mountains are closing up, losing their depth of field.

The remaining luminescence seems to be drawn to the surface of the loch. I try to imagine the passage of a single wave of light, oscillating at several hundred thousandths of a centimetre, travelling at nearly two hundred thousand miles per second, spearing straight as a die, Einsteinian curvature excepted, from the sun to the ionosphere, to the stratosphere, to the open sky of the world, through the clouds above my head, down to the surface of the loch, there to be somehow diverted northwards to its final resting place: the retina of my eye. How many such waves are flooding through my window, every second that I sit here, maintaining the colour and shape and movement of what I think I see? What would happen if they were switched off? Would it simply be the blackest of black nights, or would it signal something more fundamental?

A herring gull, still brilliantly white despite the hour, lands at the bottom of the croft. I can just make out the yellow of its bill and, with the binoculars, the red spot on its lower mandible. It wanders randomly up the croft towards me. I wonder how close it will come.

Heavier cloud is moving in from the west, darkening the loch and casting a pall of rain over Meall Ailein and the peaks beyond.

Now it is neither day nor night. I can still see the rippling on the loch and the white walls of the houses on the other shore. It is a slow and peaceful expiration. I think it may be nice to die thus, gently, without rage.

Colour is almost gone. In the twilight the cottages across the loch become more animate. Creag Mhaol and Creag an Duilisg have resolved to flat silhouettes.

Now I can see my reflection in the window: an indistinct face, lit by the blue light of a screen; two hands cradling a chin. With only a slight alteration of my focus I can see straight through myself to the other side.

*

A woman is walking a dog along the shore front. She is wearing a deep mauve anorak and dark blue waterproof trousers. Her outerwear looks bought for just this moment. The dog is a white spaniel with a single black patch on its head. It snuffles excitedly, a city dog in the countryside.

The woman and the dog are playing a game. She throws a white ball with a ball-thrower. The dog chases and retrieves the ball. The woman's throwing is clumsy and inaccurate. She abandons the ball-thrower and lobs the ball with a stiff arm. The dog chases it, immeasurably happy.

*

Two pairs of greylag geese paddle along close to the shore, shepherding their goslings. One pair has four tiny offspring, the other pair three bigger ones. The parents keep to each side of their progeny, necks low and extended in a pre-emptive defensive gesture. One of the pairs comes in to the edge of the water and waddles ashore. Their chicks, fresh-minted and fluffy, struggle over the rocks and seaweed, keeping close to their parents' sides.

After just a few seconds they return to the water. The two family groups paddle off to the east, but a minute later they are back, attended by three non-breeding adults. For a moment the whole party, seven adults and seven chicks, lies directly in my line of sight to the red car parked beside the house over the loch. They make their way obliquely across the water towards the Strome Islands, each bird rippling the surface with a faint v.

*

The early morning sun illuminates the right hand corner of my table. The candlesticks and coffee pot throw crisp shadows. The sunlight accentuates the layer of dust that covers everything.

Towards the other shore a yacht is motoring seawards, borne easily on the ebb tide. I reach for the binoculars. The yacht is called *Tiftie*. On its starboard side this is announced in large letters on a spray dodger and in smaller letters sign-written on the hull near the bow. I assume this is repeated on the port side. I wonder whether the yacht's name is also carried on its transom. The yacht is a factory produced fibreglass craft, perhaps thirty-five feet long, indistinguishable from thousands of others.

At its wheel is a bulky man with white hair. A woman is standing in the cockpit, using a pair of binoculars. She trains them in my direction. For a moment I fancy that she is looking deep into my window. I raise my right hand and wave it back and forth, slowly and deliberately. There is no response. I keep my hand aloft a moment longer before lowering it.

The yacht passes out of sight behind the Strome Islands. I watch the top of its mast as it crosses behind the islands' single bush of purple rhododendron.

*

Two couples pass along the shore searching for shells. One man is tall and thin, and steadies himself on the seaweed with a walking stick. His white hair is largely hidden by a flat cap. His partner wears a red anorak and a pink sun hat. They search at a leisurely pace. The other male is short, and shows his wife everything he finds. He decides to deposit the shells of sea urchins on the edge of the flat strip of land that borders the shore beyond the croft fence, perhaps to collect them on the way back. There is no interaction between the two couples, even though they are searching the same patch of sand and seaweed.

A few yards out on the loch a pair of mergansers is diving for food. Between dives they lower their heads into the water, searching for prey.

*

Heavy rain pummels the roof with the hiss of distant surf. It eases, and the downpipe clanks dully as it disgorges into the drain. The intermittent sound somehow evokes cowbells heard across an alpine valley.

A house fly is walking up the inside of the window. It crosses the line of the receding tide edge, moves up past the east end of the Strome Islands, and pauses directly in front of the house to my right across the loch. After several more vertical ascents it buzzes frantically against the glass but can find no way through to the world outside.

*

It is high tide. Cloud thuds in low from the south-west.

The greenery across the loch is at full burst, clothing the hard slopes and crags; life gripping the soil and striving sunwards. The lighter tones of sessile oak and rowan set off the staid green of downy birch.

I wonder how many trees there are in the world.

The firebreak behind the house and the red car has narrowed, squeezed in from left and right by billows of verdant branches. Now that it has taken hold, there is no stopping this will to propagate.

I think more about this hidden cellular frenzy. Within my view an infinity of leaves, each one the outward expression of a trillion pulsating cells, push on through their relentless cycle.

I try to penetrate this aliveness. The outward form is an illusion. I am built to see it that way. I wonder what I would find if my eyes could see past the mere shape and colour. Would it be too anarchic, too overpowering? Is it only through our limitations that we can keep the world in tolerable containment? If we had the power to see things as they really are, would we simply go mad?

Or are we already mad?

A yellow helicopter whisks across the sky, heading seawards.

Nine burgundy carriages drawn by an outsize locomotive trundle east, passing behind the houses across the loch: the Royal Scotsman. I use the binoculars to check the observation platform at the end of the rear carriage. It is empty.

＊

A piece of crumpled scrap paper tumbles across the grass in front of my window, driven on by the strengthening wind. It is out of place, disconcerting, until I realise that it is a pale pink blossom from my neighbour's azalea.

＊

The morning scene is misty with low cloud. I am startled to see the red car begin to move. It pulls out of the gateway of the house across the loch and goes slowly along towards the house to my right. By its careful progress I deduce that the track is very rough. I expect the car to stop at the right hand house, but it loops behind it and carries on, soon to be hidden by the trees to the left of the Fernaig railway bridge.

I have come to regard the two houses as a kind of pairing, despite the several hundred yards that lie between them. This is no more than a fanciful construct. I realise that I will have to be much more careful in my observation; that I will have to stick to recording what I see without allowing imagination or sentiment to encroach.

I wonder about the validity of opinion. Would it be better to live without forming a view on anything at all? Would it be possible? It is a seductive thought: to exorcise the requirement always to make a judgement; to do nothing but watch and record with strict impartiality. Would it be the greatest wisdom, to have no opinion on anything, to be content to receive impressions, nothing more?

It is too big a thought to assess in just a few minutes.

A red-throated diver works along the loch, diving just a few yards off the shore, and an unexpected patch of sunlight brightens up the narrow meadow between the two houses opposite, turning the grass a luminous apple green.

*

It is a new day and I decide to start afresh. Along the way, I have been seeing what I want to see, and believing what I am predisposed to believe.

I consider whether I ought to scrap the journal I have written so far and start again, but decide to retain it. It will be a constant reminder of the ease with which one can fall into error, and a spur to do better.

The grass of the croft is sprinkled with daisies. Towards the right-hand fence, buttercups are proliferating, and under my window some muted clover flowers are pushing through. Every blade of grass is bejewelled with droplets of morning rain. The taller daisies nod gently, shaken by the passing breeze.

*

A layer of confused cloud moves across from the east. This suggests that there is a depression somewhere to the south of us. I try to construct a mental image of the various movements in play: a mass of air gyrating anti-clockwise around a calm centre; at the same time the whole system spinning eastwards in gravitational harmony with the planet beneath it; and more than that, the whole lot – planet, atmosphere and everything

19

in between: sea lochs, baby geese, red cars, sprays of gorse and rhododendron, ladies in pink hats, fence posts, candle sticks and used copies of *Meditations on First Philosophy, with Selections from the Objections and Replies*, by René Descartes – falling through the void in its solar orbit at a speed of nearly seventy thousand miles per hour; and even more than that, the whole system moving in several planes at a combined speed of nearly sixty thousand miles per hour, to which can be added its galactic orbit at a speed of nearly half a million miles per hour.

It is hard to attribute premeditated causality to any this: my window, my chair, me, glued by the attraction of mass to a body leaving twelve million miles in its wake every twenty-four hours. The twelve million miles are meaningless: co-ordinates on the blank sheet of infinity; a half-step in an endless intergalactic waltz. The scale and wonder of it invite nihilism.

A seal pokes its head through the surface of the loch and looks to the sky. After a second or two it retires to the depths.

*

I can see the bonnet of the red car. It is parked on the far side of the right hand house, partially hidden by the house's western gable. This would seem to suggest that there may be a connection between the two houses after all. Once more I have been jumping too readily to the wrong conclusions.

In any event, the question as to whether or not there is a connection between the two houses is of no importance. It derives from the need always to find a narrative. There is no story; no beginning, no middle, no end. Objects collide or do not collide.

Having cleared my mind I feel more settled, more resolved. The journey requires more discipline than I had imagined.

I wonder about the undirected observation of random minutiae, and where it might lead. There is, after all, nothing but the accretion of detail; nothing to see but appearance.

I think about our great arc through space: twelve million miles a day. I study the leaves on the low hedge of privet in front of my window and watch the loch rippling gently in the evening breeze. Herring gulls wheel over the Strome Islands. The windows of the houses across the loch stare back at me.

*

A subdued clatter approaches from the west. It is the Royal Scotsman. I watch with the binoculars as it passes along the artificial embankment at the foot of Creag an Duilisg, over the single arch of the Fernaig railway bridge, and behind the two houses opposite and the four houses off to my left. I can see yellow lettering on the side of the diesel locomotive pulling the nine carriages. Just beyond the Fernaig railway bridge the words come into focus: *West Coast*.

I study each Pullman car as it passes. Some are less windowed, presumably the service carriages. Then come the passenger cars, windows framed with mustard-yellow curtains. I can see a regular layout of table lamps with lampshades in the same yellow.

It takes about forty-five seconds for the train to cross from one side of my window to the other. After the passing of the train the day is almost static. The low cloud scarcely moves and a steady rain lightly patterns the surface of the loch.

*

The cloud grazing the summit of Creag Mhaol drifts off to the north, revealing long streaks of diaphanous mackerel cloud interspersed with pale blue. Several great black-backed gulls spiral up high into the clear sky.

*

The loch is almost a mirror. Only the flow of the ebb tide distorts the reflections of the hills, trees and houses opposite. The white façades of the cottages, cut by the black rectangles of their windows, send long stalactites out across the water. The shadow of Creag Mhaol stretches right to the water's edge at the bottom of the croft. Between that reflected peak and the more imposing shadow of Creag an Duilisg, darkening all of the water to my right, a massive M of loch sends back an inverted representation of the sky: a luminous mix of greys, silvers and a single smear of almost-blue. Every perturbation of the surface – the flick of a fish-tail, the arc of a seal, the breast wave of a paddling eider duck – registers with a horizontal sliver of platinum.

A zephyr idles down from Creag an Duilisg, destroying the reflection of the right-hand house, and a swallow skitters across the croft, its beak overflowing with a tuft of wool.

All the interactions of the moment are gone before I have finished my attempt to record them. The light has evened to a bland uniformity, and the ruffling of the loch has destroyed the detailing of its reflections. My eye is drawn to the hills further back, where a shaft of uncertain sunlight has focused on the wooded lower slope of Creag an Duilisg, accentuating the curve of each tree and darkening the shadow on its unlit side.

That moment is as quickly gone, and now I wonder about a drift of smoke rising from the valley behind the house directly opposite.

I think again about this continuum of objects colliding, each somehow infused with its own mindless purpose. There is no progression, only an infinite circularity, a constant exchange of energy, an inexorable re-fabrication of matter.

The smoke has diffused away. Creag Mhaol stands as seemingly immutable as ever; would that I could sit here long enough to witness the grinding down of a mountain.

*

The rain has settled to a steady downpour, smudging the detail across the loch. Something odd is moving between the two houses directly opposite, travelling slowly from left to right. I reach for the binoculars. Two men are running. The one nearer the shore is wearing a luminous green top, the other a slightly darker, but still garish, shade of green. They are side by side, and viewed without binoculars seem to be a single entity making its way west. I watch this bright green blob as it passes behind the house to my right and disappears into the trees close to the Fernaig railway bridge.

*

Seneca and Marcus Aurelius lie unopened on my table, close to my left elbow. Mostly their mere presence is enough. Soon I may have to open one or the other and read some words. Even now a phrase infiltrates my inner ear:

The best revenge is not to be like that...

A fresh south-westerly wind has enticed the herring gulls to take to the air over the Strome Islands. I fix an individual bird and follow its flight path as it swoops downwind, banks swiftly round and hangs still for a second or two before somehow coaxing forward motion out of unmoving wings. It eases itself to the windward end of the islands before repeating the manoeuvre.

Another self-admonition creeps in:

No chorus of lamentation, no hysterics.

*

Out in the loch two small seals are hunting. They have found a shoal of fish: after almost every dive each one surfaces with a mouthful of writhing flesh. One starts swimming along the surface towards the bottom of the croft, carrying its prey in its jaws. I reach for the binoculars and find that the animals are otters.

It is an elementary error of perception. I ought not to confuse a seal with an otter, but I wonder whether it really matters. All animate life is fundamentally the same: a mouth, a digestive tract, an anus, reproductive organs. Exterior morphology and behaviour reflect no more than differing strategies to keep the mouth filled and the species propagated.

An otter is just a different version of a seal. I am just a different version of an otter, or a house fly, or a humpback whale. An assumed higher intelligence encourages pretensions to being something more. I resolve to see myself as no more and no less than any other form of life.

The otter, closely followed by its mate, is nearly ashore. I lose sight of it below the tall grass along the bottom fence.

*

I try not to be distracted by the obvious movement: the gulls gyrating over the Strome Islands, the sparrowhawk ploughing across my widow with a small bird in its claws, the constant ruffling of the water. I centre instead on the stillness of the trees across the loch. There is something admirable in the invisibility of their endless metamorphosis. Their will is as strong as mine, and more resilient. The same goes for the grass of the croft and the daisies and the clover; they shrug off every scything by my neighbour's mower and just keep coming. Is that real intelligence: to refrain from sentience and just get on with it?

*

The morning light is unconvincing; something is holding it back: unusually thick cloud, moisture-saturated air. It feels more like dusk, darkening as I write. My eye comes back to the veneer of grass, trees, heather, ferns and flowers stretching away to the smudge of Beinn Conchra. The strength and resilience of this greenery is an illusion. It has the most slender foothold on the sphere it partially clothes. I think about the roots of the birches opposite. How deep do they penetrate into the crust of the earth? Five feet? Ten feet? I do a calculation. Ten feet equals roughly one two-millionth of the radius of the planet. The forests opposite are scarcely clinging on. Their luxuriance is less than wafer-thin. I am struck by the raw opportunism of this abundant growth. Ten thousand years ago these hills groaned under their burden of ice. Now a verdant, comforting tide has overrun the rock. I look across at the silent trees. They have invaded all but the steepest pitches of cliff-face. They seem always to have been there; always to be there.

On we spin. I try to picture the whole sphere in its proper ratios; mostly molten core and mantle; near the surface a thin layer of floating cooled rock, above that a sliver of ocean, or in parts the pustules of crust pushed up to form the land; and this land itself, less than a third of the surface area, greened with a micron or two of vegetation. Only a niggardly concept of time and a breath-taking introspection protect us from the precariousness of it all.

*

Close inshore a procession of floating seaweed, presumably dislodged from the tide wrack at high water, moves west on the ebb tide, helped by a light breeze from the east. Each clump is bound up in a foamy brown scum. The movement of the weed is leisurely, perhaps a quarter of a knot; by low water it will have travelled another mile and a half, out into the wider maw of the sea loch. There its progress will be arrested by the turn of the tide. It will be forced back landwards, but on a different heading, and at a lower speed. Its eventual fate is beyond prediction. Perhaps it will end up stranded once more; or it might overcome the push and pull of the tides and find liberation in the open sea.

My reflections are interrupted by a commotion over the Strome Islands. A female kestrel is crossing over from my side of the loch, sending the gulls up in a defensive flurry. A flock of passing oystercatchers makes a token feint at the falcon as it nears the islands. The kestrel comes in low and for a moment I think it has landed somewhere in the vegetation to the right of the purple rhododendron. After a minute or two the gulls quieten down. I can only assume that the kestrel has carried on over the loch to scour the wooded slopes of Creag an Duilisg.

*

I remember my sea-going mantra: *if you can't see anything it is because you are not looking hard enough.* I wonder whether there is any more fruitful activity than simply to look and to listen. The rest, the hysterical activity, seems no more than an exaggerated manner in which to keep occupied; a way, as much as anything, to avoid having to look and to listen. I try to imagine a world in which everyone is still. I count the windows of the houses across the loch. There are about twenty. What if behind every window there was someone sat peaceably, observing, recording, thinking, minding his or her own business? What if that were seen as the only way to live? What if whole cities, whole nations, renounced madness and opted for an observant calm, for quiet, for stillness?

A white wagtail and two goldfinches sit close together on the twin power lines above my window, preening and scratching. The goldfinches fly off. Almost immediately a swallow arrives to join the wagtail, but only stays for a few seconds. The wagtail, now alone, balances on one leg, bobbing gently and watching the world.

I stare across the loch and listen to the silence. Only the faint mewing of a gull on the Strome Islands penetrates the glass of my window. The thought is too seductive to let go: *a world purged of unnecessary movement, a world liberated from mechanical noise.*

Creag Mhaol stands out in dark relief against a patch of lighter cloud behind. Every detail of its silhouette is engraved on my memory. On the steep fall of its western side a single tree has sprouted from the rock, creating one soft blemish on the mountain's razor-sharp outline.

*

Once more I can hear the Royal Scotsman approaching from the west. I have the binoculars ready by the time it eases into view, rumbling along the stone embankment beneath Creag an Duilisg. The morning sun is brilliant, throwing the north side of the train into shadow. The grey roofs of the nine carriages are almost sparkling.

For a few seconds I scan the train randomly, before deciding on a more controlled method of observation. I line the glasses up with the red car and the firebreak behind. The train will pass between the two at what is the closest point from my window. The side window of the locomotive is down. The lettering *West Coast* is a yellow blur, now no longer in need of deciphering. A man wearing a high visibility waistcoat is standing at the open rear door of the first carriage, looking my way. The remaining eight carriages trundle past. I can see figures standing on the observation platform at the rear of the train. I follow them with the glasses until the train is out of sight. It is a couple. The woman is wearing a dark skirt, the man a pale suit and a tie. His elbows are aloft, and at first I think that he is looking across the loch with binoculars. Somehow the angle of his arms is wrong; I realise that he is taking a photograph. I wonder, in the bright light, what is the length of his camera's exposure. My guess is that the scene will be captured in about one hundredth of a second.

*

Heavy rain, driven in by a strong easterly, is sluicing down the window. Everything beyond the glass has lost its focus. The general division of mass is still there: meadow, water, woods, mountain, six rectilinear houses, but the finer detailing has gone. Only on my side of the pane is there perfect clarity of vision. I am tempted to study the shape and texture of each point on the antler lying across my windowsill, but the effort seems wrong; it is a misdirection of my limited energy. I force myself to look out once more at the muddied view. A blur of short-lived whitecaps dances across the loch from left to right. The gulls over the Strome Islands double then disappear as they cross the fluid prisms running down the windowpane. The outline of the hills is somehow pixelated by the runs of water. The far shore of the loch too has become a knobbed, wavy line. I use the glasses to try to define a black spot in the middle of the water, but all they do is magnify the distortions.

The rain stops and within a few seconds the pane dries, apart from a few spots. The view from the window comes back into focus. I can see three sheep in the pasture to the left of the house opposite. I notice that the gorse bushes at the top of the firebreak are losing their flowers. The grey clouds drifting across have reassumed their gossamer edgings.

*

A clump of seaweed, glistening and scum-free, is carried up the loch on the last of the flood tide. I watch its slow progress. Close inshore to the left of the croft there is a back-eddy which has created a whirl of static foamy water. I wonder whether the seaweed will be diverted round into the eddy and come to rest there, but it skirts along the edge of the dead patch and disappears to the east.

A bulkier patch of weed, almost the size of a small dinghy, follows along behind. It is closer to the shore and comes to a halt at the seaward end of the eddy.

The surface of the loch is unmarred by even the faintest patch of breeze. The smoothness of the water cannot mask its flow: every imperfection is carried along north-eastwards. Once again the loch becomes a broad river, this time heading the wrong way, back up the valley to the hills.

The inverted reflection of the Strome Islands is almost unblemished: even the resting gulls are reproduced as small white pillars. The flowers of the islands' sole rhododendron are fading. The shrub is not yet absorbed back into the general greenery, but its extravagance is almost gone.

I think again about the narrative: circular, not linear; every end a beginning; every middle an end; causality an illusion built on randomness; nothing but the undirected interplay of infinite detail.

An aluminium dinghy, powered by a noisy outboard engine, intervenes from the seaward side, crossing between my window and the Strome Islands. It skims across the loch, throwing the surface into disarray. At the helm is a grey-haired man. Sitting in the bow, facing him, and sheltered from the wind by a folding spray hood, is a woman in a life jacket, dark top and shorts. The dinghy crosses towards the four houses to my left. It swings round to starboard and heads back west along the far side of the loch. Within fifty seconds of first appearing, it is gone.

*

The surface of the loch splutters and dances under the solid rain. I try to determine a suitably descriptive form of measurement which might somehow capture the play of water on water: drops per second per square metre, perhaps. I fix a small area with the binoculars. At its heaviest the rain may be producing one hundred drops per second. I calculate the approximate area of water in view: a million square yards. I am watching one hundred million drops of rain fall every second; a billion every ten seconds; six billion a minute.

It is well outside the capacity of my perceptive faculties. The quantification of what I am seeing can only be arrived at by theoretical calculation. Even when I know the figure, I cannot conceive it in any meaningful form. It is the perennial frustration: limited perception; limited intellect; limited understanding; the unbridgeable gap.

A breeze gets up from the south-south-west, setting up a train of small waves and destroying the patterning of the rain on the previously smooth surface. The air thickens with heavy moisture, reducing Creag Mhaol and Creag an Duilisg to mere shadows behind a silver screen.

*

A movement high on the slopes of Meall Ailein has me reaching for the binoculars. It is a forestry truck, hauling logs. The top half of the truck's cab is painted white. The truck is moving along the track to the north of a stand of mature pines. To the east a segment of hillside is newly razed, an oblong brown scar. The line of demarcation between the cleared ground and the standing trees is, from this distance, geometrically precise; the trees have been scythed like corn in a meadow. The truck disappears behind the foreground slope of Creag an Duilisg.

I censure myself for the ease with which I am distracted by movement and novelty.

The incessant agitation within the view from the window becomes unbearable. Heavy cloud pours across from the east; the surface of the loch shimmers as ever; the gulls circle over the Strome Islands; two young white wagtails flick and race around the grass below my window; the privet shakes in the breeze. I wish that all this motion would cease; that at the given command the world would just stop. I am suddenly convinced that a hiatus of even ten seconds in this inexorable grind would bring more enlightenment than my seventy years of searching.

I realise the impossibility of it, at any level. To cease motion is to move outside of time and therefore space. The scene and its constant bubbling cannot be frozen for even a millisecond. To stop is to die.

I focus on the red car parked at its usual spot beside the house across the loch. Perhaps if I could concentrate all my thought on that one fixed spot, a blood-red stain in a field of green, I may get closer to the calm centre I seek.

*

I contemplate the red car, feeling that my journeying has taken a small step forward. The prettiness of the view is less seductive; I am more resistant to the chance intrusions into my field of view.

Just to the right of the red car, and set a little way further back, on this side of the railway line, is an attractive tree, a perfect oval in full leaf. It may be a young sessile oak, or perhaps a rowan. I debate the relative merits of the red car and the green tree as objects of contemplation. Would not the tree, rooted as it is to the spot on which it stands, and a living organism, be a more appropriate subject? Is it not a little perverse, given this conventionally beautiful landscape, to be drawn to the one garish and transient artefact?

For the moment, the seeming artificiality of the red car, its brightly pigmented and over-confident steel, its mutability, its potential for rapid and imminent decay, hold more appeal. It is less comforting; in an hour it may be gone. It is more of a discrete object than the tree; just a thing, perishable and forlorn, disconnected from the interplay of life that surrounds it.

Conversely it is no less valid as a component of the view. To be artificial is not necessarily to be unnatural. The red car is no more and no less a construct of nature than is a swallow's nest or a beaver's dam.

The weak morning sun reflects off the body of the red car's wing mirror, creating a tiny spot of brightness visible from across the loch. The outer leaves of the oval tree glow like a halo.

I wonder whether the two taken together – green tree and red car – may contain between them all that a man needs to know. I use the binoculars to get a better sense of the detail of their relationship. A low wooden fence runs up from behind the red car to the post and wire fence that borders the railway line. The green tree is growing to the right of the wooden fence, just inside the railway boundary. Also to the right of the wooden fence is a triangular clothesline suspended between three posts. To the left of the fence, behind the car, and up against the railway boundary, is a dark green heating oil storage tank. Those are the objects which seem to define the small space inhabited by the red car and the green tree.

Our spinning has lined up the sun directly between a patch of clear sky and my window. We are past the solstice, and so the sunshine is starting to infiltrate below the top of the window frame. The candlesticks throw sharp shadows on my table, and as I type I feel the rays of the sun warming my hands.

*

Persistent rain from the south-south-east drives at the window, once more distorting my perception of everything on the other side. Only the extreme left-hand side of the windowpane, sheltered by the projecting masonry, presents a clear view of a vertical sliver of low privet hedge, wind-swept loch and the meadow, trees and cliffs across the water to the east. The red car and the green tree opposite are indecipherable.

I wonder what I am doing here, a mind presumably connected in some way to my cold hands, trying to make sense of data emitted from presumed objects, data scrambled by its passage through a film of distorting liquid, itself no more than another class of presumed object.

My only consolation is that at least I am making the effort. Logic tells me that the journey is futile, that there is no destination, and little, if anything, to be acquired on the way. One minute I see a red car, the next it is gone.

The nettles have sprung up to fence height at the bottom of the croft. For the moment there is nothing to do but watch their blurred flower heads swing back and forth in the wind.

*

Heavy cloud, bursting with imminent rain, lowers across from the south-west, scraping the summit of Beinn Conchra. A few wisps drift over the tops of the pines on Meall Ailein, in places merging into the forest itself.

I take the binoculars and study the red car and the green tree. The firebreak rises directly behind the green tree. I notice that the gorse flowers have gone and that the firebreak is now overrun with fresh green bracken.

A movement in the meadow to the left of the white house distracts me. It is a man dressed in a grey shirt, trousers and rubber boots. He is carrying a white container. He stops and pours something from the container into a receptacle which I cannot see. He puts down the container and climbs over the fence into the next small paddock, in which there are a few ewes and lambs. He makes two attempts to catch one of the ewes by driving the small flock into a corner of the field, but she eludes him. He climbs back over the fence and returns to the white house.

I put down the binoculars and wonder whether I should stop using them. They enhance my visual capacity but make nothing else any clearer. They create an imbalance in my senses. I could see the man running round the meadow, but I could not hear his panting or smell the dew and the deep odour of the sheep.

I realise that I give too much importance to what can merely be seen. It is a learned behaviour, difficult to shake off. Perhaps for a while it would be better to watch the world with closed eyes.

*

The breeze, again from the south-west, maintains the restlessness of the water. Even if I scrunch up my eyes to put the whole scene out of focus, I cannot eliminate the movement of waves from right to left.

A small yacht, fibreglass but of traditional design, motors into view heading seawards. Its mast grazes the red car as it passes. It is towing a rubber dinghy. I wait until it is out of sight before trying to pick up my line of thought.

I close my eyes and try to hold the view from the window in my mind's eye. I can reconstruct its parts, but the mental image is chaotic and unconvincing. I hope to freeze the movement, but the whole scene dances around behind my eyelids, interspersed with patches of orange and white.

I narrow down the internal image to just the red car, the green tree, the fence, the clothesline and the heating oil tank. Now I have more success. I bring myself right up to the red car and run my hand over its cold bodywork. I open the passenger door and smell the interior upholstery. I ease into the front passenger seat and gently close the door. I open the glove compartment. The car's logbook is in there, and a small torch. I close the compartment and look out of the passenger window across the loch. I can see strips of croft running down to the water, and four or five widely spaced houses. The houses are backed by a high bank of trees.

I stop the game and open my eyes. For all its amusement, it gets me nowhere to try to look back at myself.

I feel a more intimate connection with the red car. It is something I will need to think about. There are now two red cars: the one parked across the loch, and the one I have sat in. Is one real and the other imagined? And if so, which is which? Or are they both real? Or both imagined?

I can see a figure moving quickly along the track across the loch. Before I can stop myself I reach for the binoculars. It is a portly man jogging eastwards. He is wearing a white T-shirt, dark blue shorts and a baseball cap. He passes in front of the red car and the white house opposite. I put down the binoculars and watch his progress unaided. When he reaches the first of the four houses to my left he turns round and jogs back. He runs at a steady pace, back past the house opposite and along the track towards the Fernaig railway bridge. He passes behind the house to my right and a few seconds later disappears into the trees.

*

The cloud is low and solid, still streaming in from the south-west. The top ridge of Meall Ailein comes and goes behind its veil of stratus. The loch glows a dull pewter.

It would be possible for me to sketch the scene from memory with considerable accuracy. I know the exact placement of almost every tree and rock across the loch. I could make a good approximation of the patchwork of mature pines and cleared ground on Meall Ailein. I could reproduce the size and geometry of every window in every house. The contours of the Strome Islands, and of Creag Mhaol and Creag an Duilisg, are engraved in my mind's eye.

I have an intimate knowledge of what I am observing, but as yet it is still a complete mystery to me. Perhaps there is a numerical explanation for my failure to grasp the essence of what is beyond the window. My lifetime so far represents about one sixty-six millionth of the lifetime of the planet; not only have I limited faculties, I have an absurdly limited time in which to exercise them. I try to restructure the mathematics to something more manageable. If the age of the planet were just seventy years, then my allotted span would be thirty-three seconds. My eyes will be closed before they have scarcely opened. Perhaps it is unreasonable to expect even the slightest comprehension.

A freshly fledged white wagtail swoops on to the grass in front of my window. It is one of the second brood, just a few days out of the nest. Already it runs and struts with the confidence of an adult.

The trite symbolism that could be attached to the red car and the green tree has not escaped my notice. It is of no interest. They are simply two constructs, one animate, the other inanimate, which happen to find themselves in close proximity within my line of sight. They are not juxtaposed in any way. For the moment we are three objects – car, tree, me – aligned in time and space. No one of us represents anything other than itself. There is nothing sequential, no metaphor, no meaning, deliberate or otherwise.

I look across at the car and the tree, stolidly holding position as we whirl along. A white sheet is flapping in the breeze on the clothesline in front of the tree. The random movement of the sheet is hypnotic. I am only assuming it is a sheet. I resist the urge to pick up the binoculars to check. It may be a large white shirt, or a towel. The precise definition is irrelevant: it is white cloth hung on a line and snapping vigorously in the wind. For the moment that is all that matters. I feel a great peace watching it. Its movement is accentuated by the stillness of the red car and the green tree. I start to sense the weight of years that have led to these few seconds; the infinite series of cause and effect that has produced a moment of which I am part. I have no real idea what I am or how I come to be here watching woven and freshly laundered material billowing on a line, or why I should find some element of repose in that distant movement.

It is calming and strengthening. I suspect that a mind concerned only with the immediate and present beauty of white cotton dancing in the wind might have within it the seeds of invulnerability,

*

37

A rock pipit abandons its territory down on the foreshore and perches for a second or two on one of the twin power lines stretching above my window. I record the moment, for that is my task. I start to feel a certain cleavage in my perception. Perhaps I am a little less absorbed by the randomness of the detail; perhaps now I sense a little more strongly the great circular rush of interaction, the overpowering and chaotic madness of matter.

*

Creag Mhaol and the bank of trees behind the houses opposite are in deep shadow, but the morning sun lights up the eastern slopes of Creag an Duilisg and the higher, secondary shoulder of mountain beyond. Up there above the treeline the rock is carpeted with a sward of fern and heather. It might be good to be up there in the bracing morning air, looking back down at the loch and at the lines of extravagant peaks to the north and west.

I stifle the thought; I have, after all, been trying to exorcise the need to be always seeking the next titillation, however seductive it might appear. I have more than enough within my current line of sight. To underline the point, a cloud moves between the sun and the mountain top, darkening it to little more than a silhouette.

The back edge of the cloud shadow moves across the high moorland to the south of Creag an Duilisg, allowing the sun to revive the vegetation. The light catches the tops of the trees on the bank behind the houses opposite and creates a dappled mosaic of green on black. Off to my left the loch sparkles in a shaft of morning brilliance.

*

A layer of high stratus has dulled the day. Only the water is restless. I try to apprehend everything beyond the window as a single entity, rather than as an agglomeration of parts. All I am looking at is the same fundamental matter in one of its manifestations. Everything is interchangeable. Everything is provisional too, except matter itself. Even the Ancients understood that matter is both indestructible and finite in an infinite world.

I look at the sheer cliffs of Creag an Duilisg and the trees clinging to every ledge and couloir. I watch the ebb tide emptying westwards, the swallows strafing the grass of the croft, the dots of sheep in the meadow to the left of the house opposite. I think about all of this in relation to the strongest hypothesis of the moment: that nearly fourteen billion years ago all matter was compressed to the size of a pinhead before exploding outwards to form the galaxies, the stars, the planets and, in time, mountains, trees, lochs, swallows and sheep. It may be, too, that once the centrifugal forces are exhausted, all matter will once more implode back to that pin head, before recommencing the whole process.

Perhaps all I am looking at is one version of an infinite series of universes.

It is helpful to try to think in these broader terms. It puts our spinning and our twelve million miles a day into a more appropriate context. The matter which makes up my own body, mutable but indestructible, always has been and always will be a component of this great expansion and contraction. For the moment the cells of my body have combined to provide a certain level of sentience, allowing me to observe, for the briefest of moments, the process in action. That sentience will soon fade, but my components will live on, in a different, more diffuse form, permanent participants in the cosmic carousel.

A collared dove lands on one of the twin power lines and sits low, its belly almost touching the wire. I study the subtlety of its shape and coloration, the fineness of its black bill, the softness of its eye. It takes to the air again and with intermittent, rolling wing beats heads off across the loch.

*

Once more there is a dislocation between the winds of sky and surface: the clouds stream across from the south-east, directly in line with my window; the waves of the loch are pushed by a wind from the south, breaking obliquely on the shoreline below the croft.

My mood, too, is dislocated. There are times when I have to force myself to look through my window, times when I am discouraged, tired of the whole business. At these moments I lose the sense of what I am observing. The scene becomes flat, one-dimensional, irritating. The great shoulder of Creag Mhaol mocks me with its stillness and its solidity. I know that it will be ground down and reworked and shifted bodily across the face of the earth, that in the scale of things its ephemerality is scarcely less than my own. Nonetheless I am tempted to turn away, to abandon the hard work, to find solace in triviality.

The wind gusts more strongly from the south, sending dark patches scudding across the surface of the loch. Wavelets tumble forward with a flash of white. The gulls over the Strome Islands hold themselves head to wind, wide-winged and almost immobile.

I try to find my way back into the substance of the day, softening my mind, suspending thought. I stare at the waves breaking on the shore and let them wash over me. I let my eye drift along the intersecting lines of hills stacked behind hills, imbibing no more than the rough geometry of a shifting landscape.

It is no good. I am too conscious of the glass of the windowpane. For the moment the clouds and mountains and water are impenetrable. I start to wonder why they should ever be considered uplifting or beautiful.

A hooded crow perches uncertainly on the fence at the bottom of the croft, wings stretched to keep its balance in the breeze. It gives up and drops down out of sight beyond the nettles.

I continue my watch-keeping, aware that I have no choice.

*

The rocks at the north end of the Strome Islands are dotted with herring gulls. The gulls are always there, standing patiently, or crouched down in smoother nooks or patches of grass. Only a sea eagle will drive them up into a screaming flurry. This year's fledglings try out their wings, flapping skywards a foot or two and drifting back to earth.

The cloud thickens from the south-west, driving the rain in harder.

The gulls align themselves head to wind, eyes cast westwards towards the open sea, minds empty of yearning. They are unburdened by the heaviness of time. I wonder how it would be, to rest naked on the crust of the earth, blown by wind and rain, watchful of nothing but the now.

*

The morning is so still that for a moment I doubt our spinning and wheeling. Only the faintest loom of the sun behind a veil of cloud argues for the idea.

I realise that I am caught in a no-man's-land: incapable of knowing total quietude; unable to feel the thrill of our flight through the void. The two extremes of stasis and motion are beyond reach. All that is possible is a half-baked meditation and the dragging around of a leaden body. There are two possible directions of travel; both are circumscribed.

I stare through the window, watching a slim column of smoke rise vertically behind the bank opposite, the sole movement apart from the shimmering of the loch. I am imprisoned behind the window, but if I stepped through into the world nothing would change: the glass cage is inescapable.

A family group picks its way along the edge of the shoreline, from left to right: grandfather, young couple, granddaughter. The grandfather is wearing a blue sweater and carrying a camera. He arranges the others for a photograph. The couple hold their daughter between them at shoulder level. She is wearing a fleecy pink top. The grandfather crouches down, framing the trio with the peak of Creag Mhaol. He records the moment and the group moves on.

The sun burns through the haze, throwing shadows behind the low clumps of privet close to my window. The day reassumes its air of stillness. I watch it with a suspicious eye, aware of the mendacity of appearance.

*

Two harbour porpoises make their way up the middle of the loch on the flood tide, drawn in by sea trout and salmon. They roll forward gently, snouts scarcely breaking the surface, fins a brief black sickle against the silver of the water.

I think about the proposition that the making of those fins was laid down in a pinhead of matter fourteen billion years ago. I try to find a way to calculate the number of molecular reconstructions required along the way. The possible trajectories are too numerous to pin down but must surely be in the billions. I think about it again and suspect that even that may be a gross underestimate. Perhaps it is hundreds of trillions, or even more.

For the moment I settle on a trillion molecular metamorphoses to create the path from a pinhead of matter to the fin of a harbour porpoise. I wonder whether each of those transitions is a necessary cause and effect, making the fin an inevitable outcome; or whether some or all of the transitions are a matter of chance.

I put the question into a different form: *if an identical pinhead of matter, in an identical state, were to explode in an identical way, would the result be identical?*

On the assumption that every cause has its necessary effect, the answer would seem to be yes, but it would take only a single infinitesimal variation in the first cause to throw everything onto a completely different track. Perhaps if one single atom out of the zillions and zillions compressed into that original pinhead had occupied a fractionally different position, the structure of the resultant universe would be quite different.

The porpoises disappear up the loch to the east. I try to make some sense of what I have been thinking about, of the probability that here are porpoise fins slicing the water, and that here am I observing them. It seems to be an inevitability based on chance. Once the roulette wheel has been set in motion the outcome cannot be changed; everything depends on the push of the wheel.

I realise why I have no option but to sit at my window recording what I see: it is my inevitable function in the whirl of universal matter.

*

The day is cold, grey. A jumble of unfriendly cloud blusters its way in from the south-west. The wind murmurs and bellows in the eaves, presaging a likely storm. I search for some relief in the momentary desolation. The rhododendron flowers have faded away, along with the gorse. The green of the woodlands across the loch has lost its freshness. Only a stand of gold-of-pleasure, a tight-packed smear of waving yellow squeezed between the long grass and nettles at the bottom fence, prolongs the brief optimism of the growing season. Summer has not yet come but seems already to be turning on its heels.

*

As I travel, I shrink. My mind broadens, but at the expense of my sense of self. My relationship with the view from my window is calculable; but with everything that lies beyond I am ground down to less than nothing. My physical and temporal dimensions shrivel away; I start to penetrate the illusion of self-determination. This progression neither offends nor surprises. It is liberating to confront one's own absolute insignificance.

*

A few sheep dot the steep pockets of pasture on the mid slopes of Creag Mhaol. As they move around, the patterns they create on the hillside evolve, introducing a modest sense of movement into the landscape. Sometimes they disappear entirely under the trees or reappear in a new location. I count sixteen sheep in widely spread groups of nine, three, two and two. It is the trio and the two pairs which have ventured the highest, grazing their way onto the most precipitous ledges.

*

I maintain the hard work of recalibrating my sense of scale. It is perhaps the only way to escape the numbing parochiality of the planet. I suspect that if I could achieve some ease with geological time and galactic distance, my travels would be more fruitful. If I could feel, not just intellectually, but viscerally, the reality of arcing through space at twelve million miles a day for a billion years; if I could conceive of the full stretch of five hundred billion galaxies, each of a hundred billion stars; if I could picture myself travelling at the speed of light for a million years simply to link two neighbouring coordinates in the vastness of the sky; if, too, I could reduce myself to my true relationship with the infinite plane of the universe; if I could do all this, then perhaps I could start to escape the infantile, the small-minded and the cloyingly terrestrial.

Swollen clouds, heavy with latent menace, pile in from the south-west. Their upper edges, caught in a dazzle of sunshine, tower skywards in foamy confusion. An expanse of milky blue opens up. I project myself upwards and through it, racing beyond the clouds, beyond the blue into the cool, indifferent black. Now I am at the speed of light, watching the planet recede astern. It shrinks to a pinpoint and is soon lost in the lightshow of a billion stars. I settle down with an easy mind, ready for a million years of tumbling through the void.

*

It is low tide, and the loch is as still as I have seen it, disturbed by only the faintest undulation. The reflected landscape has as much depth and substance as the water itself. It is impossible to discern exactly where the exposed rock of the Strome Islands ends and where its reflection starts; the inverted image is almost faultless. The denuded brown of the rhododendron bush is faithfully reproduced on the surface of the loch.

I contemplate the twin images: the supposedly real landscape and its illusory double. Their respective realities seem equally valid; both are no more than the play of light on my retinas.

A rain shower clouds the surface of the loch, fusing the fine detail of the reflection into no more than smudged blocks of colour. The real landscape could be lost just as easily. The difference in the respective substance of object and reflection is no more than a matter of degree.

The rain brings a faint breeze that silvers the water, destroying the reflected image. Returned to the singular, the landscape loses its vibrancy. I think about the pathos of the ephemeral and the fragile.

*

The pre-dawn sky holds no more than a few wisps of high cirrus, their eastern edges growing pink as we revolve towards the sun. The silhouette of Creag Mhaol looms crisply black against the lightening sky.

I feel a strong urge to count days. My own, so far, number twenty-five thousand one hundred and sixty-four. The planet has known nearly six trillion. There I am forced to stop: before the formation of this spinning sphere of rock there was no basis on which to calculate the length of a year or a day or any of their derivatives: these are purely earth-bound concepts. I am not inclined to apply our local and short-lived measure of time indiscriminately. To take time back to the birth of the planet may itself exceed what is strictly rational. If one accepts the Kantian contention that nothing can exist without an observer, as it is only a sentient onlooker who can impose time and space and causality, then the concept of time immemorial has no foundation. In whichever direction one projects, our days are numbered.

The sun is still not visible, but its rays now strike the upper rock-face of Creag an Duilisg, transforming the fractured geology into a riot of sparkling gneiss pitted with deep shadow. I notice that the peaks of Creag Mhaol and Creag an Duilisg are currently in alignment with the sun: I can watch the rounded shadow thrown by the former work its way down the woods on Creag an Duilisg's lower slopes.

The east-facing rock of the Strome Islands finds the sunlight next, creating a horizontal streak of brilliance across the dark blue water of the loch. The gulls crowding the western end turn to face the light, and a little way beyond, on Eilean an t-Sratha, a cormorant spreads its wings to dry.

*

There are not six houses across the loch, but eight. A low unpainted building next to the right-hand house, which I took to be a barn, is in fact an old cottage. The long house furthest to my left is not a single building, as my perspective suggested, but two cottages side by side. Nonetheless all I can see clearly are five white and one pink single-storey structures. The idea of six houses, even if incorrect, is so firmly established that for the moment I am reluctant to let it go.

I feel better for having put the record straight but wonder whether there are other aspects of my travel notes that may be equally erroneous. The task of recording what one sees is not simple.

*

The wind is from over my left shoulder: from the north-east. It is odd to see the clouds, still grey and laden, heading back towards the south-west; the day has a back-to-front feel.

I think about our direction of spin and wonder whether it could have been otherwise. What forces initiated the eastward gyrations? I try to imagine a world in reverse, spinning towards the west: dawn over the Atlantic; sunset behind the hills; weather systems inverted.

I realise that it is not true to say we are only conscious of our spinning at an intellectual level. The pattern of our relationship with the sun is somehow infused into the psyche. Maybe it goes deeper than that, into the fabric of the body. Perhaps we are physically responsive to magnetic fields and gravitational pulls.

A patch of faint morning sun strikes the moorland behind Creag an Duilisg. I try the mind-game of shifting the light to the western edge of Creag Mhaol, thrown by a sun rising in the west. The disorientation is complete; I feel a slight frisson of vertigo. Such a world would have to be relearned from scratch.

The exercise is instructive. I realise that I am much more attuned to planetary movement than I thought. I am as much participant as observer; our direction of travel has a strong and necessary hold over me.

We spin and wobble with unerring predictability. The tides come and go to a stable rhythm. We arc through space on a sure trajectory. It is all seductively comforting.

Heavier cloud rolls in from the north-east, flattening the light. I cannot see the sun, but I know where it is, as I always do.

*

The red car is parked in its usual spot just to the right of the house directly across the loch, passenger side towards me. It is the first thing I check when I survey the scene. A small, covered trailer has appeared to the car's right, in front of the oval tree. I have no choice but to accept its presence but would prefer it not to be at that exact spot: it intrudes into the pleasing triangular relationship between car, tree and clothesline. I realise that there are aspects of the view towards which I have become proprietorial. Familiarity has led me to wanting things to be a certain way. I feel a tiny stab of annoyance at anything that is slightly out of kilter.

In fact, not every intrusion is unacceptable. I see that four sheep are grazing on the firebreak. I enjoy watching their changing configurations. Sometimes one or two disappear under the trees on each side of the break. This gives rise to a game: will they reappear higher up or lower down? They all disappear and the firebreak returns to its usual state.

I think a little more about the trailer parked near the car. It is probably eight feet long and six feet high, and is a silver-grey colour. It is therefore a clearly visible rectangle. I wonder whether, if I were painting the scene, I would include it or not.

I try to draw my thoughts away from the trailer by tracing the profile of the hills from left to right. I am rewarded by noticing for the first time a tiny, rounded peak tucked away in the crook of the angle between Creag Mhaol and Meall Ailein. It is a fair distance away, perhaps as far as Beinn Conchra to its south-west. Somehow, I had previously seen it as part of the middle ground of Meall Ailein. I open the Ordnance Survey map and have no difficulty locating the peak: Creag Mhòr, four hundred and seven metres high. This unexpected expansion of my horizon gives me a rush of pleasure. The tiny sliver of hillside draws me out in another direction. It is almost a twin of Beinn Conchra, just a few metres lower and the same distance away. At the moment Beinn Conchra is hidden behind cloud, but Creag Mhòr is sharply defined. It is set behind a narrow declivity in the wooded slopes of Meall Ailein, and so is hung around with a necklace of pine trees.

*

It is high tide, reducing the Strome Islands to a thin horizontal. The weather is once again from the south-west, promising wind and rain; already a few drops streak my window.

I am undecided where to start. Within a few seconds various options have presented themselves:

A description of the various sheds across the loch, as yet unmentioned.

A description of the sailing dinghy and small motorboat currently occupying two moorings in front of the five houses off to my left.

A description of the heron flying at a great height over the middle of the loch.

A description of the three herring gulls displaying with shallow wingbeats and raucous calling at the bottom of the croft.

The heron and the gulls have the most immediate interest, but they are gone in a few seconds. The boats across the loch will have a little more longevity within the scene, but they too will soon be gone.

The sheds comprise:

A large green agricultural shed set a little way to the right of the house directly opposite.

Three small sheds of rough construction, two of corrugated iron, one of timber, clustered around the two houses to my right.

My thinking is interrupted by the blue workboat, the *Toohey II*, which passes between the croft and the Strome Islands, heading seawards. On its deck is a pile of rusty chain and a huge anchor, suggesting it is off to lay a mooring somewhere. The garden bench is still there, visible behind the pile of chain.

I struggle to overcome the ease with which I am diverted by the new and the ephemeral. The *Toohey II* is of no lasting import; nor is the flight of a heron or the style of cladding of a garden shed. The houses will crumble, as will the hills. I can now see that the sheep on Creag Mhaol have reached the highest slopes; one is grazing above a precipice of rock. Sheep and rock will all go, each in its own time.

There is nothing, absolutely nothing, that I see on which I could have a permanent hold. There is nothing visible that might give a sense of an indestructible essence. The more I look, the more I see insubstantiality, impermanence and a magnificent senselessness.

My eye is forced back to the water, to the arm of sea stretching past my window. For all its constant agitation, it is the sea which holds the biggest promise of permanence, but even that is a kind of illusion: two parts one gas, one part another. Even that will go when the sun reaches its final throes, heating the ocean to a boiling cauldron and sending its components back into the ether.

*

I am not sure where these travels are leading. It is not that I have lost my way, but that my destination seems to be changing. I am learning more than I expected. The more I examine the view from my window, the less substantial it becomes. I have a little less care for my own mortality. The envy I felt for the great buttress of Creag Mhaol and its seeming indestructibility has evaporated. I am on a par with the mountain; each of us is no more than a brief and equal expression of the force of matter.

*

All the herring gulls are up off the Strome Islands, circling in a frantic mob. I suspect a sea eagle must be close. I search the sky for the tell-tale silhouette and find it, a little off to the west: not a sea eagle, but a great skua. Its soaring is laboured: every few seconds it gives a few rapid flaps of its white-flashed wings. It makes its way off to the north-west, circling as it goes, leaving the gulls to resettle on their rock.

Two minutes later the gulls lift off in one body. Instead of holding station above the islands they head over the loch towards my window. There are perhaps two hundred of them, filling the sky almost above my head. Mixed in with them is a tight flock of oystercatchers. I pick up the skua again, high up and heading across the loch towards Creag Mhaol. It circles several times over the shoulder of rock. As I watch it I look for sheep, but there are none. The skua flies a little way further up the loch, then turns and once more makes its way seawards.

The gulls return to their quiet occupation of the islands except for a single bird that lands on the corner fencepost at the bottom of the croft. It preens for a while, and then watches the world with sharp head movements and an impassive yellow eye.

*

A single-minded ferment of life; all the possibilities put to the test. The underlying will of the universe transformed, on this one mote in the eye of infinity, from the inanimate to the animate. Everything a necessary conjunction.

I think about the binary nature of it all: one is either in or out; on or off; one or zero, with no choice for the one, limited choice, if any, for the zero. There are only participants, no onlookers, no third parties. Participation is only from the inside out.

I realise that I am no more than a temporary current thrown by the switch of causality. My free will is an illusion. I wonder whether gratitude is in order, or not. Should I be thankful for the opportunity to sit at my window, trying to make sense of the impenetrable maelstrom of matter? When I return to zero I will have no memory; it will never have happened; it may as well never have happened. I make no difference to anything; nothing makes any difference to me.

3

The dew is autumnal, glistening under a sun set squarely on the window. I have contemplated the solar angle so long and so thoroughly that I can feel the shift of our spin as something palpable. Perhaps if I keep at it I may engage viscerally in our fall through space. For the moment, though, I must find my way back into the substance of the landscape.

I note so many changes:

The gulls on the Strome Islands have thinned to just a few birds.

The clumps of privet under my window have greened and sprouted.

The seed-heads of flowers and grasses along the bottom fence are now brown and brittle.

The woodlands clothing the lower slopes of Creag an Duilisg wait in silence for the turn and fall of their leaves; for the first time I sense a majesty in their close-bound patience and the sureness of their rhythm.

The lower sun now provides a fierce backlight to the silhouette of Creag Mhaol, creating an outline so crisp and black that it seems disassociated from the softer hills around.

A spotted flycatcher has adopted the right hand fence for its hunting station.

The houses opposite, for the moment subsumed into the shadow of Creag Mhaol, have lost their detail and their familiarity: I cannot be sure whether or not the red car is parked in its usual spot; the firebreak behind merges blackly into the woods to each side, indistinguishable.

I make an inventory of the scene and start to feel calmer and more open. It has become more than a friend, almost a necessity.

*

I caution myself against attachment. I have only my mind, and that I must let go willingly when the time comes.

*

A few insubstantial clouds hang almost immobile in a sky of rinsed-out blue. I watch them closely and see their fronds of vapour form and unform. Within a minute or so a single slight cloud, hanging low over Beinn Conchra, has split into four ragged wisps of white. These four subdivide, and within another minute the cloud is gone.

*

It is only through this landscape that I can find my way back into the thread of my thought. It holds within it as much as I can possibly know, little though that may be. There is no great secret to be found in this trinity of sea, sky and mountain; it teaches nothing but itself.

The wind has died away, leaving only the out-flowing tide to motivate the water of the loch. Beyond the bottom fence a lone goldfinch feeds on thistle heads.

I could love this landscape and the myriad components of its life. I know that I must not. Better simply to absorb its underlying silence and serenity. Better too to be wary of its comfort.

A military jet passes high overhead, heading south-east. Its precise vapour trail intersects the gossamer threads of cirrus fanning out from the south-west. I hear the rumble of the jet's engines until it is lost to view over Meall Ailein.

It is difficult to deny the insanity of the human condition.

*

I fight against the frivolity caused by absence. For the moment my eye is too taken by passing detail; I have to learn again to by-pass the immediate and the obvious. My head still swirls with the inattentiveness of the mob.

The red car is back, a calming centre on which to focus. In the flat morning grey of an imminent storm, the car's dull carmine is scarcely discernible from its dark green backdrop. Nonetheless it provides a point of rest.

I contemplate this smudge of pressed metal across the loch. The more I look, the harder it is to see. The morphology of the vehicle disintegrates. For a moment I fancy I apprehend it as it really is: no more than space and electrical charges in an unbroken continuum of the same. I can see right through it, through the soil and rock behind, essentially all the same, through the base of Meall Ailein, on further through soil and vegetation and out into the sky beyond, piercing the atmosphere at a tangent, all, all the same: space and charged particles without substance.

I realise that I have a line of sight which stretches to infinity in whichever direction I care to travel. There is no reason to be circumscribed by the limitations of the retina. My mind can see whatever it wants to see. For the moment I am simply one point in the infinite agglomeration of space and particles, essentially indistinct, but capable of projecting my mind, and therefore seeing, in any direction. I understand now that my true vision is spherical, not linear. I have eyes not just in the back of my head, but in the top, the bottom and the sides.

The thought makes me light-headed. I am neither subject nor object; that is no more than a crude differentiation. There are no subjects, no objects, only a unified sea of energy. The rearrangements of that energy are no more than provisional and ultimately inconsequential.

In quick succession four fluffed-up redpolls perch momentarily on the power lines above my window, five rock doves flash their white rumps as they pirouette in formation over the loch, and a buzzard lands on the gatepost at the bottom of the croft. The buzzard lifts its tail and sprays the grass with a stream of excrement.

*

For the first time I feel that I am starting to get somewhere. There is no order to my thoughts, no sequential neatness, but this does not matter. My process is one of random accretion. Slowly I am starting to make connections. I strive to be rational, but not strictly logical. Pure logic leaves little room for the serendipitous insight, for the corner-of-the-eye *aperçu*.

*

The wind thuds into the house: a low sustained roar interspersed with momentary crescendi. That, and perhaps the clatter of rain on the window, is the one tolerable intrusion into the silence. There is something primeval, sidereal, in this rush of air. It is the wind we should by rights feel as we career through space. It puts me in mind of solar winds, of hurtling meteorites, of the wheeling perturbations of the stars and planets. It signifies endless displacement. It recalls, too, storms I have known at sea: raw, elemental, barely survivable. It is the undertone of the universe, this driving wind, the music of the spheres, the one legitimate accompaniment to the whirl of a zillion atoms.

A flock of twenty or so twite, tossed by the gale, find refuge on the grass of the croft. There they gorge themselves on the wilting heads of self-heal, laying up fat for the winter ahead.

Now the rain starts, streaking obliquely across the window. The broken sky suggests a sharp squall, no more. I close my eyes and tune in to the timeless grumbling of the wind.

*

The buzzard is back, perched this time on the bottom left hand corner post, and attentive to the long grass around it. It is a dark-plumaged variant, rough sooty-brown with a mayoral chain of lighter pigment across its breast. The bird is facing away from the loch, its back towards the southerly wind and the piercing morning sunlight. It must see my face illuminated behind the window. I am tempted to feel some complicity with the bird as we share the moment, but resist the notion. It spreads its wings and drops heavily down into the grass close to the post. It fumbles for a few seconds and I suspect a kill, but it takes to the air again, bill and talons empty.

I think about the constant reassembly of matter. My component atoms will one day soon revert to the common stock, thereafter to be spread wide into the world. The worm will eat me, the thrush will eat the worm, the buzzard will eat the thrush. I will be diffused back into the stream of life by a million channels. I will end up disaggregated, a little bit of almost everything.

I try to project the other way, to imagine the past trajectories of all the atoms that compose my body. My constituent parts have been on the road for fourteen billion years. What stories could each one tell! My cells, too, are constantly renewing. Every day I acquire a new batch of atomic backpackers. For many I am just a bed for the night.

I realise that I am no more than the transient sum of a million genetic encodings: cells and atoms provisionally harnessed to serve the idea of *me*.

I am happy that having been thus assembled on a knife-edge of probability, I will, on dissolution, make an everlasting contribution to the future world. That will be my afterlife.

The sun sears low into my window and turns the loch into a blaze of molten gold. I scrunch up my eyes to be able to look straight along the blinding corridor of sunlit water and lose myself in a lightshow of shimmering stars.

*

A pall of misty rain drifts across from the south-west, turning the hills over the loch to no more than looming shadows. On the damp grass below my window, white wagtails race and dart from one titbit to the next. One hovers for a second in front of my window and lands on the sill. It looks in at me with a black impenetrable eye. Motionless, we stare at each other. I can feel its wildness. We are separated by just three feet of distance, thirty-six inches of the infinity of the universe, but the chasm of our genetic divergence is seemingly unbridgeable.

I realise that it is only the glass between us which has emboldened the wagtail. Thus contained I am not a threat.

The bird makes a lunge into the corner of the window frame, disposes of the insect that has brought it there and flicks away in a blur of grey, white and black.

*

The tilt of our spin still moves towards the north, bringing the sun into my window at a more direct angle and lengthening the shadows of the low clumps of privet lined up a few yards in front. Every year for a few billion years the planet has tilted this way, and then reversed back, always within the same span of movement. I wonder what would happen if the tilt just kept on going, putting us into a permanent spin on two axes. One year I would look out to the Arctic, the next the Tropics, the next the Antarctic. Sometimes the sun would be to the south, sometimes to the north. Life would be turned on its head. The regular and restrained tilt of our orbit is just one amongst an infinite number of sustaining improbabilities.

*

The morning is infused with a dull silence; even the light is flat and featureless. I notice the first hints of brown amongst the trees across the loch. The leaves are beginning their slow death. I will watch as they fall, soon to be absorbed back into the mulch of life. I will reflect on this inescapable rhythm and rehearse my own death a million times as I watch each leaf spiral downwards.

A sudden squall darkens a rough oval of water and sends it scuttling across the loch to the shoreline at the bottom of the croft. A second or two later I hear a rumble as the gust reaches my window. The taller shoots of privet judder and bend.

The wind passes and a flock of chaffinches swoops in and lines up on the right hand fence. The birds are too heady with autumn restlessness to stay there long: they chase and fight, feed for a moment on the grass, and quickly hustle off.

*

I take up my position behind the window and try to evoke once again the sensation of molecular fusion with everything around me. Before I have had time to conjure up an image of a porous epidermis, only loosely demarcated from its gaseous surround, the blue workboat, the *Toohey II*, chugs past. One crew member is occupied shortening the lines of the fenders dragging in the water. Another is sat on the garden bench, fixing something small with his hands. Beneath the bench are two diver's oxygen tanks.

I start again but the moment is lost, and I wonder anyway whether the effort is worth it. Perhaps Epicurus was right; perhaps I should abandon this senseless journey and give myself over to the pleasure principle.

I close my eyes. I can feel the thudding of my heart, the pulse of blood through my arteries. It carries on irrespective, beyond my control. My mind tells me that all this stuff is mine, but I am not so sure. I have no meaningful ownership of this provisional arrangement of matter which I am pleased to call myself; there is no title in perpetuity. How, then, can I lay claim to anything beyond my own tenuous boundaries? Is the window really *mine*? Am I typing on *my* computer? Is this *my* oil lamp, *my* candlestick? The notion of property, of proprietorship, suddenly seems absurd. I may just as well assert title to the wind now humming in the eaves.

The cloud thickens from the south-west. Across the loch the red car holds together, still playing its role. The privet shakes and the waves angle in towards the shoreline. The hands I consider mine tap keys on a keyboard. I watch it all as we spin and drop into the universal emptiness.

*

For a moment the sun is blinding, even though I am wearing a peaked cap to counter its lower elevation. It is almost impossible to look at the loch; the reflected light is too strong. A mass of cloud piles in, moderating the glare, and leaving a single shaft of sunlight to illuminate the woods on the eastern slopes of Creag an Duilisg. Within a few seconds the bubbling green is transformed to an indistinct smudge as a rain squall sweeps through. A tight flock of rock doves spirals down to the shore below the croft.

Every second sees an infinity of transformations; indefatigable energy empty of purpose.

The cloud and rain pass and once more the sun streams into my window. I feel the deceptive comfort of its warmth. One day it will flare and die, taking with it all the gods and sorceries.

A herring gull bobs gently a few yards from the shoreline, pushed eastwards by wind and tide, and dabbing at the surface kelp. It passes through the shaft of reflected sunlight, and for a few seconds merges into a furnace of molten gold.

*

We spin on, away from the sun, away from the day. The pale blue sky, untroubled by the least cloud, unblemished to infinity, is tinged at its lower rim with a faint glow of pink. The crags of Creag Mhaol are infused too with a roseate blush, softening their hardness and their angularity. The faint shivering of the surface of the loch is not enough to undermine the sense of stillness.

As the light fades the air becomes grainy and opaque, somehow distorted by a residue of unseasonal warmth. The sun is long gone, but a hint of refracted pink colours the whitewash of the houses across the loch. Even the water, flooding in from the west, seems to have taken on a softer tint.

I would be happy, right at this moment, for the spinning of the planet, and the orbit of the moon, and the wheeling of the sun and stars, to stop; for the great orrery of the universe to grind to a halt; to enjoy, just for a short while, some respite from this incessant motion; to freeze this moment; to savour a little longer the half-light, the poise between day and night.

There is no stopping, no respite. Already the hills have blackened and the sky has faded to the colour of slate. The motion is inexorable, relentless, maddening. There is no point of rest, neither at any place nor at any time. My heart beats and my blood pulses, every second of every hour of every day, and the globe spins and the moon orbits and the stars fall through space. Nothing can be stopped or slowed or diverted. It goes on and on, a treadmill turning round and round and round, forever and forever and forever.

We have spun on into the night. The moment, if it were ever there, has gone, to be replaced by another and another. I snatch at them but they dissolve before they are caught, chimera left fading on the path behind.

Two slugs of light traverse the blackness across the loch: the carriages of the Plockton train. They pass like distant meteorites, no more embodied than shooting stars.

*

Nine swans, adult, pure white, wings surprisingly supple in motion, fly west, almost at the height of Creag Mhaol. For a moment they redefine the scale of all things avian: nine birds filling the sky, drawing the day into themselves. Too heavy with majesty and innocence to allow indifference, they pierce my heart.

*

For days, perhaps weeks, I have travelled in almost total silence, doubting the utility of even a single word. The bubbling of an oystercatcher working along the tide edge is no less cogent than the constructs of language, and no less enduring. Fifty, a thousand, a billion words get us nowhere; they will never stop the stars in their tracks.

Perhaps from here on I will write with the swirl of a fingertip across a blank page, the movement of the hand as valid as the flow of ink or the intoning of syllables. It is an appealing thought: words dancing in the air, invisible; unseen words thrown to the sky; words liberated from sense and structure; words unbound from their masters; words left free to make their own journeys.

I know it will not happen. My travels are inevitable and pointless, and I must swaddle them in words.

I look across the loch. The red car is there in its usual spot. I have no choice but to continue. Even though there is no narrative, I must search for the end of the story.

*

The dying of the leaf cover destroys the uniformity of the trees across the loch. The leaves of the rowans maintain a weak hold on life, clutching at a fading green. The birches have given up the struggle; their leaves have slipped away into a sere russet the colour of distant stags. Only the sole rhododendron on the Strome Islands sustains a brash and brassy sheen.

It is still a mystery, this ordering of organisms without mind; their sureness and purpose. Lack of thought or sentience in no way diminishes the force of their will. The trees, the grasses, the sedges, the flowers, the fungi, the lichens and mosses, all these growing things, they just keep coming on and on with a silent and unthinking determination. There is something heroic in their relentless adherence to their task. Their rhythms are more sure-footed than those of man; their probe and retreat more measured, more stoical. They are more absorbed, too, into the physics and chemistry of the whole, stretched as they are through a continuum of light, air and earth. They draw sustenance and give sustenance in equal measure; their balance sheet is clean.

The mid-morning sun, diffused by a haze of high stratus, is now halfway down my window. The Arctic-facing slopes of Creag Mhaol and Creag an Duilisg brood in unrelenting shadow, and the trees which clothe them draw themselves in, ceding their leaves to the long hibernation ahead.

*

The more I travel, the more the shape of my thought moves away from the linear. This eternal spinning has infected the geometry of my observation. It has thrown me into a kind of orbit, a long, parabolic sweep that carries me off into distant recesses then hurls me back into a close pass of the central gravitational mass. My thoughts follow this uneven trajectory, and so are loosely circular. At each close pass I may, if I am lucky, see something worthwhile, only to be hurtled off into the blackness. Sometimes the orbit is concentric, sometimes eccentric. It is dizzying, unsettling.

I am now resigned to this randomness. Perhaps I may in time become a kind of quark, capable of occupying two points in space simultaneously.

*

Fifteen or so redwings, unmistakeable winter heralds, swoop over the window from behind and spiral down to the grass of the croft. I admire the boldness of their colouring. They have probably been flying all night, fleeing the northern snows, but they are still restless; the drive to be getting on south has consumed them, and within a few seconds they are off again. They have a clear pre-dawn sky of the palest Wedgwood in which to make their way.

I think about the falling of the leaves and the displacement of the birds: motion and transformation driven by the tilt of our travel; each will-to-live finding its own solution to our move away from the sun. All this easy action, honed to near-perfection through millennia of trial and error, makes me feel lumpen, mal-adapted. There is a loss of connection with the basic and the primeval. Why be so rooted to the spot by brick and concrete? I should be following the swallows and the redwings, stick over shoulder, bread and cheese wrapped in a bright red cloth, heading for the sun over hill and dale, whistling my way to warmer climes.

The sun breaks cover directly over the peak of Creag Mhaol. The glare is unbearable, and I shield my eyes with my hands.

Across the loch the water steams with a thin layer of mist. A constant and un-rhythmic rumble announces the passage eastwards of the locomotive and nine carriages of the Royal Scotsman. The piercing back-light has de-solidified everything beyond the water, and so I can scarcely distinguish the train. It passes, no more than a silver spectre through a haze of unfocussed matter.

*

The approaching season gears itself up. I remember a line:
Winter unbundles a sack of storms...
Despite my window's distance from the water, the gale
has smeared it with a layer of salt spray, turning the landscape
mucky and diffuse. Gusts still shake the house, but the night's
worst is over. The smaller birds hide from the blast; only a
few hardier types carry on as usual: a lone black-headed gull
struggling west; a mistle thrush holding position on a fence
post at the bottom of the croft.

We swing through space, taking our weather with us.

A second black-headed gull, it too in winter plumage, black-
eared rather than black-headed, labours to make progress
against the wind, angling obliquely across the loch in the
manner of a ferryman crossing a strong stream. A third follows,
and I wonder what has caused this sudden flight seawards.

Nothing is knowable, save the narrow and the parochial.
My eyes penetrate through the salt spray which disfigures
my window. The clarity of the scene is gone, but I question
whether it was ever there.

A fieldfare muscles strongly across the croft, arcing over
the fence towards the nearby rowans.

*

The leaves across the loch, now well into their death throes,
burn with a fiery bronze. It is their last gift to the one world
which I can see; a final noble hurrah.

Only the conifer plantations set with unnatural precision
on the more distant slopes of Meall Ailein maintain their
brooding green.

The loch itself is filled to overflowing, reducing the Strome
Islands to no more than wafer-thin outcrops. The water laps

almost at the roots of the rhododendron bush and the few stunted downy birches that eke out a life on the islands' topmost contours.

Bit by bit, I am becoming as sedentary as the trees, renouncing unnecessary movement; *a sphere rejoicing in its perfect stillness.* The wheeling of the bigger spheres is motion enough.

The light of the day advances, and now I can see the patches of bracken set amongst the trees, stippling the forest with the deep chestnut glow of dying fronds. Rain spatters the window. The wind backs to the south-east, sending the high-water waves straight into the shoreline at the bottom of the croft.

Beside the white house across the loch, the red car sits in silence.

*

Seven sheep from the common grazing invade the croft, gorging themselves on grass and privet leaves. One stands in front of my window and looks in at me. Its eyes are vacant, stupid.

I quash my reactive sense of superiority. Human hegemony will decay as surely as the leaves across the loch. It is a natural imperative that flowerings are short-lived.

*

I stare out of my window and drown in the deep gold of a fading landscape.

*

A small flock of chaffinches spreads itself along the right-hand fence and moves on. The air is emptying itself of birds:

the siskins have gone, and the twite, and the wagtails and the meadow pipits.

Perhaps, when the indestructible material of my body had been broken down and redistributed, a molecule or two of what is now myself may find its way into the green of a siskin's tail feather, or into the eye of a twite, and so transport me on those wild, unfathomable circulations.

I realise why I do not want god, or paradise, or heaven: they are superfluous to the perfect mechanics of matter; to ask for more smacks of gluttony.

A ball of brown hits the window at an oblique angle. I stand up and peer over the sill to make sure it is not injured. It is a wren, now on its feet. It flicks its tail and bobs. Its colour matches that of the bracken fronds crisping and dying on the slopes of Creag an Duilisg.

4

As some of the philosophers would have it, the ideal of life is the species; it is for the species that the individual, of little account, lives and dies. A man grows out of the species' will-to-live, and is subsumed back into it; so too for the oak, the buzzard, the sheep and the stag.

I survey the landscape in front of my window, blackening towards winter; shrivelling, dying; and think of all the species now extinct. I venture the thought that those great minds were perhaps in error, as species themselves live and die. If there is no permanence in the species, then it cannot be part of the underlying infinity of life. That is something broader, more pure; monolithic.

It is a double-edged thought. It negates me as a man, as anything essentially different from the robin hopping on the lawn in front of my window, or the bracken fronds now glowing a deep chestnut across the loch; they are brother and sister to me; but in that same idea resides a great liberation: it unshackles me from grandiose delusion.

A shower of rain, heavy with winter, drives through from the west. I watch with a more benign eye the drops streaking across my window. Each tiny sphere of water holds the promise of life; each one is a latent world. Part of me came from such a drop, and to such a drop part of me will return.

A seal undulates along the surface of the loch just a few feet off the shore. It seems to hold its snout in the air to smell the day before arcing downwards.

*

The nub of Beinn Conchra, barely visible above the most distant slopes of Meall Ailein, is pale with a first dusting of winter snow. I try to count the months since I last saw it thus, but wonder why I am making the effort. It is of no account. Whether I sit and watch the evolution of the landscape for a hundred days or a hundred years I will not transcend the boundaries of my own understanding. The mistake, unavoidable, is to link everything to time. My knowledge cannot operate outside of its slavery to the second, the minute, the hour. To be time-bound is to be circumscribed; imprisoned. Only death will expunge time, and then it will be too late to understand.

An otter is hunting in the deep pool towards the Strome Islands. I watch it each time it surfaces, chewing its prey to the rise and fall of the rough waves scudding in from the west. Its throat glints pale in the hazy sunlight.

*

The wind has swung round to the east, bringing with it a misty rain that smudges the finer detail of the landscape. The trees and bracken across the loch, withering towards winter blackness, are fused to one dark sweep. Only the rocky perpendiculars of Creag Mhaol and Creag an Duilisg, now a dull pewter, break through the monotone.

I reconsider the problem: *how to escape time?*

In essence the answer is simple: I must close my eyes and suspend all thought. I must lose, too, the sense and weight of my body. I must lose consciousness of self. I must, in other words, sleep an un-waking sleep, or die. I realise that to be subject to time and constant transformation is the key clause in the contract of life. Oblivion is the only escape from grinding causality.

There is an after-life: the matter of my body is, after all, indestructible; but it will be no different from the before-life. If there is any regret, it is only this: that the sensation of lying outside of time is unknowable.

The wind strengthens from the east, reinforcing the sense of our spin in that direction. By rights the wind should always be from the east, a blistering hurricane of a wind, scouring the earth as we hurtle around and along. Perhaps it would be better thus. It might remind us more forcefully that we are perched on a tiny projectile whirling at supersonic speed into an infinite night, and so jolt us out of our smug introversion, and puncture our overweening claim to specialness.

*

The ravens are down from the tops. There is little for them up there now apart from a bitter wind and ice-cold rock. I can hear one grunting as it scours the shoreline beyond the bottom of the croft. Disturbed by the sheep working along the common land, it rises and glides east on the wind. Within a few seconds it is back. It perches on a bottom fencepost, an ebony silhouette against the silver-grey water of the loch. It leans forward and croaks twice, opening its mandibles and showing the outline of a black tongue. Its upper bill is overgrown to the point of deformation, recalling the broken nose of a heavyweight boxer.

A gust unsettles it, and with a few supple wingbeats it drifts up the croft and disappears past the house to the right of my window.

*

In the washed-out dawn light I struggle with a question: *might it be possible, in some way, to have consciousness without time?* There is no answer. Within my own framework of experience, the proposition is impossible. Consciousness equals thought and sentience, which equal sequentiality, which equals time. Whether there may be another basis for knowledge, operating in different dimensions, constructed on different grounds, which somehow allows the combination of what seem to be exclusive concepts, is something I can only guess at. The fact that I cannot conceive of a concurrence of consciousness and timelessness does not rule it out. That inability may be no more than an expression of my own limitations.

I watch the waves in their endless undulations, lifting the seaweed massed close to the shoreline from the recent storms. It is only their movement in time which gives them meaning. One thing would seem to be obvious: consciousness outside of time would have to dispense with form; it could have no visual content. By the same token, sound and touch and smell would have to go. That leaves nothing but the mind stripped of its external sensors, operating in the purest of modes. Outside of time, it could not think in the simple syllogistic manner which we take as thought. Its manner of functioning would be quite different: circular, or spherical perhaps; at all points in time simultaneously, never at any particular point in time, and therefore outside of time; all-knowing, all-feeling, but without differentiation: pure knowledge; pure feeling. I try to grasp a sense of how this might be, but it is beyond me. My own thought and imagination are too leaden, too earth-bound.

Headlights across the loch divert my attention. The red car is pulling out of the double gates of the house directly opposite. It turns onto the track that runs along the shore and makes its way slowly towards the Fernaig railway bridge. Two herons in line astern fly low along the loch, just beyond the edge of the croft.

A new thought arrives from an oblique angle: if everything, as we are told, comes from a pinhead of compressed and therefore unified matter, there is a logical beauty in that proposition. It suggests that all this differentiation – red cars, herons, waves, windows, writers – is only provisional; that in the long run unity trumps fragmentation.

A herring gull glides in on unmoving wings and lands neatly on a breakwater post projecting just a few inches above the rising tide. It hops down into the water and paddles around, inspecting the seaweed for anything edible, bobbing gently to the waves.

*

The journey is growing more difficult. The landscape is pulling itself in; losing its bounty. The days become niggardly, ungenerous, as we move away from the sun. I am forced to look more deeply into the nature of things; to consider more fundamentally the motive force behind the trees now standing dormant across the loch; to wonder what drives on the shags scouring the frigid water; to penetrate the hard rock of Creag Mhaol and the snow-laden cloud drifting in from the east.

The mortification of the world is no more than a tactical retreat: the will-to-life has largely withdrawn from the surface, but in its darker recesses it fizzes and burns as strongly as ever. Somewhere inside the atrophying branches of the birches clinging to the slopes of Creag an Duilisg, branches now denuded, sap-free, frozen to a temporary necrosis, lies a hot, indomitable impulse. Nothing, it seems, will dissuade this impulse from persisting. Even death is no more than a provisional setback, signalling a reordering of energy and matter into countless new arrangements.

Winter brings a greater sense of that death. It is a move away from the light, away from the false comfort of a warming sun. The questions become starker, more brutal, the answers more opaque.

The landscape has not yet reached total stasis. Across the loch a few leaves still cling on, especially on the lower and more sheltered slopes, mottling the woods with sprays of dried-out yellow. The clumps of privet in front of my window maintain, for the moment, their greenery. The grass of the croft, cropped short by sheep from the common grazing, is almost past re-growth.

The world is hunkering down, the better to surge back when the time comes.

I remind myself that all this is no more than a localised phenomenon. It is all that I can apprehend in any meaningful detail, but relative to five hundred billion galaxies, each of a hundred billion stars and their uncounted planets, it is next to nothing. My apprehension, too, is moderated by my own mode of seeing and thinking. It is tempting, but perhaps dangerous, to draw too many generalities from one small stretch of water and its surrounding hills.

*

I watch the first snow of the winter, driven by a light easterly wind, as it frosts the grass of the croft. The blizzard thickens, blotting out the far shore of the loch and reducing the Strome

Islands to a faint smudge of grey. The ground in front of my window is soon carpeted with a solid layer of white broken by only the tips of the tallest stems of grass.

*

I think about the fact that the animate springs from the inanimate, that an appropriate cocktail of matter, under the right conditions, will create a living, reproducing organism. This suggests that there must be an *a priori* disposition, or will, towards life in the seemingly dead or inert. The transition of matter from un-living to living cannot be a mere accident; the laws of nature are not so frivolous.

Could it be, then, that every atom of the phenomena which make up our universe harbours the will-to-live? That the hard rock of Creag Mhaol burns, at the heart of its atomic structure, with a latency to life? That the interface between what appears to be dead and what appears to be alive is a fluid, open border? That life itself is merely a surface bubbling of the inbuilt propensity of all matter?

I watch the water of the loch, the colour of pale slate under a lowering sky, and enjoy the expansiveness of that last conjecture. In it lies an awful sense. The animate rises out of the inanimate, and dies back into it, to be revived in another form at another time; but the drive to animation comes not from the animate – that would be sequentially illogical – but from every component of all of matter. The will-to-life is a *sine qua non* of every atom of the universe, embedded in the form of its energy. It is difficult to imagine how life and sentience could arise otherwise.

A hefty squall buffets the side of the house and sends a spray of rain across my window. My perception of what I see has shifted a little; I feel more conjoined with what once may have appeared inimical.

I am losing interest in the houses across the loch. For a long time they absorbed my attention, but now I scarcely notice them. I am not sure whether this is because their unchanging presence has made them over-familiar, or because my focus has shifted away from the surface detail of the view towards what may lie concealed beneath it. In any event, there is more to be learned from the evolution of the oaks and birches, and from the relentless flow of the tides, than from a few square metres of harled stonework.

Nonetheless, it is instructive to come back to these structures after a kind of absence and consider them afresh. I see them now as the outer shells of vulnerable organisms. Like the carapace of a crustacean, they serve to protect soft bodies from the ravages of the world. They provide a sense of permanence and invulnerability. Like shells on the beach, though, they will in time be ground down to the finest of grains.

I consider the house directly opposite and wonder whether the relative extravagance of its design is out of scale with the mundanity of its inhabitants; whether we ascribe too much to ourselves, and whether in this are sown far and wide the seeds of hubris.

The rag-tag flock of village sheep works past the house to feed on the croft. Their stupidity has not denied then an enviable level of self-sufficiency. They are unconcerned with mortgages, three-piece suites and problems of plumbing. They have learned to convert humble vegetation into the thickest of woollen coats. They never need a bed for the night. Perhaps more importantly, they take no more than they need.

A pair of goldfinches swoops down onto the grass in front of my window. They peck at a few seeds and hurry off.

*

The colour of the trees across the loch has faded to a dark burnt umber. Only a patch of rhododendrons encroaching on the lower slopes of Creag an Duilisg retains a hint of summer green.

*

I think more about this will-to-live which, logic would imply, is the ground of all matter. Its corollary is the will-not-to-die; the two exist in stark juxtaposition, two sides of the same coin. The first is unsought, the second unseemly.

We are told that release from worldly care is to be found in the negation of the will, that there lies the road to sainthood. But to overcome the will requires a superhuman effort of that same will. There is no escape from willing, or from its necessary concomitant, action: even to do nothing is to do something.

I consider my own inaction. I sit all day and stare through a pane of glass. From time to time I type a word or two. This would appear not to be much, but it is nonetheless a forceful act of will. I take it a little further and try to discover the source of this will. Where does its centre lie? Is it located in my conscious thought, in the superficial working of my mind; or is it something already pre-formed and immutable, rising into my consciousness as an inescapable cause? I suspect that it is the latter, that I can only act as I am predisposed to act, that there is little, if any, room for negotiation with the demands of the underlying master. This subconscious will, the true heart of me, provides the ineluctable motive, while the conscious mind debates the issue and provides the necessary rationale. In this way is the semblance of free will maintained.

I watch the low clouds scudding from the south-west over the peak of Creag an Duilisg. I know that I have as little choice in the matter as they do. This is not in any way a distressing thought: my own will would seem to be predisposed to the diminishment of the ego.

The clouds race on by; moisture condensed out of thin air, pushed along willy-nilly by currents of that same air; provisional, evanescent. It would be an act of vanity to consider my own brief span more material than theirs.

*

An otter swims west just a few yards off the shore. It dives and I wait for it to reappear, but I don't see it again.

*

The crags loom blacker and the wind blows more bitterly. The distant peaks are once more patched with white. I am thankful for a world thus circumscribed; beyond those peaks men murder men for chimera.

Another squall lashes across the loch, darkening the water with a press of air. Icy rain beats on the roof and frosts the grass.

I sit, hands clenched under chin, caught in the sensuality of the moment.

*

The early morning air has a frigid, unwelcoming look, inviting me to think more about the negation of the will: the renunciation of life as a route to some sort of eternal quietus. It is a path strewn with contradictions, vain in both senses of the word. It aims for a state which can never be known. It presupposes, too, some kind of transmigration, a progression of lives to be escaped from. It is yet another variant of the denial of mortality.

A coal tit searches the grass for titbits. I search my mind and find no hint of a former life, no sense of an über-me, no trace of a soul. I can be certain that my mind is the working of my physical brain; beyond that, everything is mere conjecture.

The total negation of the will may well be impossible; but the will's many malignancies are amenable to control. The difficulty is to find the opposing will to assert that control.

The coal tit flits away, but within a few seconds is back again, this time at the base of the privet. Its perfection of form is a kind of marvel.

*

The tilt of our travel has brought the dawn sun to the centre of my window. It pierces a stream of unkempt cloud low above Beinn Conchra, creating spots of brilliance, fringes of gold. A new arrangement of the cloud creates provisional beams of light that splay across the sky above Creag an Duilisg and move slowly east, illuminating air, moisture, emptiness. A single wide shaft subdivides into a dozen smaller ones which cut with geometric perspective to the very top of my window. Within a few seconds the play of light is gone as the sun subsides back behind the darkening cloud.

A small speed boat cuts across the loch from east to west but fails to draw my attention.

*

I absorb the true nature of the view from my window by closing my eyes and listening to the ceaseless soughing of the wind in the eaves. Everything is encapsulated in its restlessness, its insistence. Fresh from my bed, I could sleep again to the rise and fall of its passing. Sometimes it pauses, filling the air with a heavy silence, an unnatural stillness. It gusts in more strongly with a rushing tremolo; a meaningless, eternal vibration. It is without structure, without harmony, scouring away the nonsense of the actual. It is perhaps the one sound which could accompany the dead in their timeless anaesthesia.

*

This landscape, this examination, this constant journeying are exhausting me. I stare with tired eyes at the grey loch and the two ravens gliding across the croft. A faint patina of light rain mottles my window. There is no escape from the absurd; no reconciliation with what is and what must be; no alternative but to endure with as much grace as can be mustered. It is wearying to search for a point of equilibrium, to balance the insanity of ceaseless striving with the need for repose. One is inescapable, the other unattainable.

The red car pulls out of the gates of the house opposite and moves slowly along the track towards the Fernaig railway bridge. In the dull light it is scarcely discernible. Its presence and movements no longer hold much interest: I am, after all, trying to assimilate the world at the level of the molecule, the atom, the proton, the electron, the positron, the quark; or even more fundamentally, at the level of its invisible will, rather than its external forms.

The sheep graze slowly along the shoreline just beyond the croft fence, unperturbed in their round of eating and shitting. A phrase from Montaigne creeps in:

Tout le monde fiente; les rois et les philosophes, et les dames aussi.[1]

---

1 *'Everybody craps; kings and philosophers, ladies too.'*

Man is as bestial as the rest.

*

The greylag geese are back: fourteen of them, feeding on the frosted grass at the bottom of the croft. I wonder how many of them are this year's goslings, and whether they find anything pleasurable in their drive to survive and breed in an inimical world. Their apparent companionability is broken by frequent mock attacks with lowered necks: assertions of ranking within the flock. Between tiffs they work away at their cold, tasteless fare, heads bent to the task.

I try to imagine the apprehension of the world without vocabulary, without any structured differentiation of its forms or actions. The geese do not conceive of themselves as eating grass. They do no more than recognise the form of an object which requires a certain action.

A goose raises its head and looks out towards the loch. I attempt to recreate its view of the landscape I know so well. For the goose it is a physical structure without any points of reference: no north, south, east, west; no geographical location; no nomenclature for loch, house, mountain, sky; no formal sense of distance; no relationship to the rest of the planet or its galaxy or the billions of galaxies beyond; no method of describing its qualities; no aesthetic, no politic; no past, no future.

The goose is quite possibly much closer to the heart of life. It must have only the vaguest sense of the division between subject and object, and is therefore more integrated into the continuum which envelopes it.

Something impels the flock into the air. The geese rise up heavily, gaining traction with their winter-pale wings, and move off to the east in a chorus of cackling.

*

The pre-dawn sky, marred only by a few wisps of charcoal cloud, glows a pale blue-green beyond the clear-cut ridges. Up to the right of my window a single planet is drawn towards the window-frame by our spin and fall.

I settle my eye on the exact spot where I think the sun will first appear, and wait. A few streaks of cloud turn pink and then silver. For a while it seems as if our movement has stopped: the sun sticks below the horizon. Only the faintest evolution of the light gives any clue that dawn is imminent. A cloud or two turn fiery, but without revealing the sun's exact location. I suspect that I may have placed it too far to the west but cannot be sure. I wait, eyes fixed on the silhouettes of Meall Ailein and Beinn Conchra, determined to catch the exact second of the sun's appearance. A small patch of cloud burns so brightly I can no longer focus on it. Still the sun does not arrive.

Then I see it, pushing up in the declivity between the two peaks, except that it quickly disappears to the east; it was a low cloud irradiated to brilliance by the proximate sun.

Half an hour passes. Perhaps the sun is now so low that I will not see it at all. A belt of heavier cloud moves in from the west, its edges on fire, and now I know that I have missed the moment. The sun is surely there, but hidden.

For a whole morning I wait.

5

There is no project, no plan, no meaning; nothing but matter, whatever that may be, compelled to action. There is no reason why the animate should be any more subject to a moral overlay than is a mountain, or a loch, or a fencepost. Chance intelligence and greater awareness argue only, perhaps, for a modicum of respect for the material, for a wish to create the least harm. Even that relativism is suspect: in a universe of five hundred billion galaxies, and perhaps billions and billions more, which endures for billions of years, or perhaps forever and ever, no human influence, whether benign or malignant, is of the least import.

There is no paradise to be created here, no paradise to be sought elsewhere. Man will continue to create his own purgatory, not through any collective malice, but simply as slave to the insuperable tide of causation. He will fight and scrabble his way steadily towards the inevitable tipping point and then, like the dinosaurs, he will go his way.

There is no reason why this assertion should be seen as bleak: it is no more than an acceptance of the nature of things. The purity of naked truth has its own charm. This planet was not created for man or for any other life-form. It is no more than one infinitesimal sphere of cooling rock amongst countless others hurtling across unimaginable distances. To ascribe intent or meaning or specialness to the aleatoric and provisional appearance of one species amongst millions on one rock amongst billions is to take credulity too far.

The wind scuds in from the east, roughening the cool silver of the loch. On the Strome Islands three hooded crows take turns to harry an encroaching buzzard. The buzzard lands in the thick vegetation midway along the main island; the crows take up position in a leafless shrub just above the buzzard, hunched aggressively, beaks pointing down at the intruder. The buzzard tires of the attention and takes to the air, winging back over the loch towards the shoreline below my window.

*

Snow lies in a wide patch just below the distant ridge of Beinn Conchra; the trees across the loch have reached mid-winter stasis; the rear lights of the red car work along the track towards the Fernaig railway bridge.

I think more about morality, conscience, virtue, good, evil; all curious concepts imposed *a posteriori* on the mechanics of matter. There can be no absolute good: all benefit derives from a counterbalancing debit; in a closed system this must be so. The idea of a transcending virtue holds no traction against the unstoppable flow of cause and effect; the system, wherever its driving force may lie, is inescapable.

The breeze, still from the east, blows lazily across the loch, summoning up the occasional patch of white foam. I watch the ruffling of the water and remember a long-held wish to catalogue every wave on every ocean in a grand *Encyclopaedia of Waves*. It seems as worthy an endeavour as any other.

Helped by the silence of the landscape I scour away the illusions. My place in this world is thus redefined, diminished, cleansed.

*

The wind persists from the east, driving sprays of cold rain onto my window.

I wonder if, when I close my eyes for the last time, it will be the image of this loch, and these hills and woods and islands, which will carry me through to death.

My window has framed a world; contained it; distilled it.

However long I sit here, the essence of what I see will not change. That essence is immune to the temporal. If I can grasp on to it, then I too may find immunity from the pettiness of time.

The buzzard, once more attended by its three hooded crows, lands on the shoreline below the croft. The crows swoop in, aiming pecks at the buzzard's back. They perch on the posts of the old breakwater and voice their displeasure.

All four fly off to the east.

*

Something disturbs the group of ten or so shags feeding on the loch. They take to the air and describe large circles low over the water, their movements untypically agitated. I search the limpid pre-dawn sky for the silhouette of a sea eagle but can find nothing.

The shags disappear behind the Strome Islands and I settle once more to wait for the sun. The solstice is not long past, but already I can sense the changing impulse of our spinning. The increasing glow of the sky suggests that the sun will appear directly in my line of sight, at the precise mid-point of my window. The sky is clear of the least cloud; nothing now can impede the capture of the exact spot and the exact moment of the sun's revelation. The halo of fiery silver just to the west of Beinn Conchra grows more intense; I narrow my eyelids to cope with its brightness. When the sun arrives, the speed of its ascent is startling. Within scarcely a minute its full diameter is exposed, blinding me as I try to assess its rate of progress. For a few seconds there is an almost perfect alignment between my window, the western peak of Meall Ailein, and this gaseous inferno. I close my eyes and lift my face, feeling already the sun's warmth, its unthinking beneficence. I project myself forwards and out, through the window, across the sky above Meall Ailein, across a hundred million miles of space, and pierce the heart of this unworldly conflagration. I fly to its centre and try to absorb a notion of its insanity, its outrageousness: atomic activity gone berserk; matter reacting at the limit of possibility for aeon after aeon; nuclear confusion of the highest order, somehow contained and resolutely spherical; an explosive residue; a kind of accident; propagator of life on this planet. I envelope myself in its searing white heat and feel the cells of my body fuse into the great thermal dance.

*

Trails of mist drift across the valley behind the firebreak, wrapping the near-black conifers in a diaphanous scarf. The subtle evolution of the shapes and shadows is mesmerising. Nothing appears to move, but within a minute or two the relationships between trees and moisture have transformed completely. The mist evaporates, revealing the starkly crude plantation. I attempt to will back the brief fog and its beautifying obscurity, but it does not come.

*

A tentative realisation starts to grow: I feel a great complicity with this landscape and its forms and its life because I came from its matter and will return to its matter. The division of subject and object is provisional and misleading: everything I see has the potential to be part of me; I have the potential to be part of everything I see. Individuality encourages misapprehension. I think again about the mortification of the self, not as a path to transcendence, but as an acceptance of the constant transformation of all matter and a rejection of the eternal soul. To hanker after life evermore is irrational and selfish. To want nothing and to give oneself up, not simply without complaint, but willingly and happily, to the incessant round of integration and disintegration, would seem holier than a million supplications for admittance to the supposed heavens.

*

In the pre-dawn half-light a lone woodcock is feeding from west to east across the croft. I have no choice but to use the binoculars to bring some sharpness to the dark blotch working in twists and turns and short runs across the pasture. It labours with total concentration, piercing the earth once or twice per second with its long bill. For all I know it has been at it all night, probing for the soft-bodied life that will sustain its own.

Rain drums softly into my window, blurring the view. The light is strengthening almost imperceptibly, despite the heavy cloud. The woodcock stretches its wings, flaps once or

88

twice and resettles them. It carries on feeding. I watch it for another minute or two. With a speed and lightness all at odds with its dumpy profile, the woodcock rises vertically and with rapid, shallow wing beats flies round the west side of the house towards the bank of trees behind. I check my watch. Its departure time is within a minute or two of yesterday's and the day before yesterday's.

I reflect on the bird's self-sufficiency, its self-containment, the genetic imperative which has infused it with such discipline and precision. I cannot avoid the over-arching question: *why*? There is only one answer: *because.*

*

Some quirk of the light has turned the layer of cloud over Meall Ailein to pale lilac, infused here and there with a silvery pink. The soft restfulness of the shade is juxtaposed by the brittle rock of the dark crags beneath.

A male merganser lands messily on the loch just below the croft. I study its exaggerated cresting and its bill honed by evolution to a sleek rapier. To my prejudiced eye the bird's physical form hovers between the sublime and the comical. The merganser lunges forward, displaying to an imaginary partner, and takes off rapidly across the loch.

The lilac of the cloud sinks to an everyday grey.

*

A blizzard drives steadily in from the east. The snowflakes are the size of small butterflies, their flight as erratic in the swirling wind. I play a game, picking out single flakes high up amongst the thousands streaming past, and watching their tracks as they weave earthwards. The wind pushes them sideways; gravity forces them down. From time to time the wind manages to lift one for a few feet, but the pull of the earth is too strong to resist.

Across the loch, white roofs now top the white harling of the houses.

The snowflakes keep coming: millions of them, perhaps billions. I wonder how many snowflakes have fallen from the sky since the cooling of the planet; how many will fall before our star gives out.

Two greylag geese paddle from right to left just a few yards off the shore. They seem untroubled by the cold, the wind, the persistent snow. They move along at an easy pace, absorbed effortlessly into inner texture of the landscape.

The cloud lifts a little, revealing the slopes of Creag Mhaol, now transformed by snow and ice to something unknowable.

*

I realise that my window has taken on a new role. It now does more than frame what I see: it protects me from it too, and so distorts my participation in the world I am recording. I should take a stool and a notebook and sit in front of the window for a day or a week or a year, fully exposed, uncosseted, and thus make my travel journal. I suspect myself of a kind of fraud. It seems presumptuous, to describe a frozen hillside from the comfort of a heated room.

I think about it a little more and see that this is a symptom of the universal difficulty: point of view; relativity. Were I to shift my chair forward just six or seven feet my perception of the world would alter radically.

I decide to redefine my terms of reference. The title of my travelogue should be: *Travels Through a Window, From the Relative Comfort of a Heated Room, Thereby Inducing One Specific Perception of the Outside World, Valid Within Its Own Particular Limitations, But Acknowledged By the*

Author As Being Something Other Than the Work That He Might Have Produced Had He Moved His Chair Forward Seven Feet.

❋

Once more the clouds, moving in heavily from the west, are at variance with the southerly wind on the loch. I wonder at what altitude these two flows of air intersect. Is there a band of turbulence between them, or do they rub along cleanly in their opposing directions? Perhaps the flow swings round progressively from one direction to the other. Rain starts to fall, complicating the mental image I am trying to construct.

The day grows gloomy. I watch the headlights of the red car across the loch as it pulls out of the double gates and moves off towards the Fernaig railway bridge. The low level breeze falls away; perhaps it will soon turn westerly. A cormorant lands in the water just a few feet off the shore at the bottom of the croft. It ducks its head under the surface and dives almost immediately. The water there is shallow, no more than a couple of feet.

Now I hear the rain on the roof. I fold my hands under my chin and stare at a grey universe. Only the last hints of snow on the furthest slopes offer any relief.

❋

A slug has appeared on my window, towards the bottom left-hand corner. It is about two and a half inches long and a quarter of an inch wide. Against the light it is a pale fawn colour, with its dark digestive tract visible through its body. I fancy I can see a looping track through the raindrops on the window that brings the slug to its current horizontal position.

The slug extends an antenna and waves it around,

searching for something: a sign, a message, inspiration. With no visible physical effort it starts to move towards the left side of the window. After edging along an inch or two it changes direction and starts to descend vertically. Sometimes it pushes out both antennae, sometimes retracts them. The fluid metamorphosis from spikes to normal flesh, then back to spikes, is fascinating to watch. I cannot remember whether the spikes have eyes at the end.

The slug turns back on itself, bringing its head level with its tail. Its front half is now lying alongside its back half, almost side by side. There it pauses, bent double against the glass, forcing me to the conclusion that there is no hierarchy of wonder. Every last thing is an undiluted miracle.